THE REVELATION
OF THE MYSTERY

WITNESS LEE

Living Stream Ministry
Anaheim, California

First Edition, June 2002.

ISBN 0-7363-1687-1

Published by

Living Stream Ministry
2431 W. La Palma Ave., Anaheim, CA 92801 U.S.A.
P. O. Box 2121, Anaheim, CA 92814 U.S.A.

Printed in the United States of America

02 03 04 05 06 07 08 / 10 9 8 7 6 5 4 3 2 1

CONTENTS

PREFACE

This book is composed of messages given in Chinese by Brother Witness Lee in a young people's training in the church in Taipei on September 1-5, 1975. These messages were not reviewed by the speaker.

Chapter One

GOD'S ETERNAL PURPOSE

Scripture Reading: Eph. 1:5, 8-11; 3:3-6; 5:17; Col. 1:9b; 2:2b;
1 Cor. 2:7; Rev. 4:11b; Rom. 12:2; Matt. 6:10

THE MEANING OF THE UNIVERSE AND HUMAN LIFE

The verses listed above show us God's eternal purpose, God's eternal plan. Everyone needs to know God's eternal plan. If as a young person you are somewhat thoughtful, you do not need to be a great philosopher to eventually ask questions such as, "What is the meaning of my life in the world?" and, "For what purpose was I born?" If you consider even further, you might also ask, "Why do the heavens and the earth exist? Why does the universe exist?" If you give a little thought to these matters, you will discover that the meaning of human life cannot be found in clothing, food, housing, or transportation. You will also conclude that the meaning of the heavens, the earth, and all things cannot be focused merely on human living. These conclusions, however, reveal only what the meaning of the universe and of human life is not. It is difficult to determine a direct answer to the questions concerning the true meaning of the universe and the true meaning of human life.

If we want to find the definite answer to these questions, we must look in the holy Scriptures. Today there are millions and millions of books in the world. However, there is only one book—the Bible—that clearly explains the meaning of the universe and the meaning of human life. The Scripture verses listed at the beginning of this message are the answer to these questions. If we would thoroughly get into these verses, we would see the meaning of the universe as well as the meaning of human life. We would see why the universe exists, why human life exists, and why we were born.

These few passages from the Scriptures tell us that God has a plan. A purpose is a plan, and a plan is a purpose; however, *plan* may be a better word than *purpose*. God's eternal purpose is God's eternal plan. The word for *plan* in Greek has the sense of "beforehand." A purpose, design, or plan exists before the actual event occurs.

In brief, God's eternal plan is that the universe, including the heavens, the earth, and a myriad of items, would be a background or backdrop and that the center of all these things would be man. Man is the center of the universe. God's plan is to gain a group of people to be His corporate expression. God desires to have an expression for Himself, and He wants this expression through man. God's desire is not to be expressed through angels nor through any other creature but to be expressed through man. Furthermore, He does not want this expression to be through an individual man but through a corporate man. Therefore, God's eternal plan is to obtain a corporate man to be His expression in the universe. How will He obtain a corporate man as His expression? He will do so by dispensing His life and nature into this corporate man. Hence, He ordained that this man should have the sonship. God planned beforehand and foreordained that we would receive the sonship, that is, that we would be born of Him and become His sons, having His life and nature.

This matter is absolutely unrelated to man's fall and his acts of sin. If man had not fallen and sinned, and even if Satan, the devil, did not exist in this universe, God would still desire to carry out this matter. This is because God's purpose, God's plan, is that the heavens, the earth, and all the myriad of items in the universe would be for the existence of a group of people whom God would regenerate to be His sons and who would have God's life and nature. Although God is divine and these people are human, God's divine life and nature would enter into them so that they would possess His life and nature. He would be the Father of these people, and they would be His many sons. Thus, they would receive the sonship not for the enjoyment of abundant blessings but for the expression of God.

CHRIST AS THE EXPLANATION OF GOD
AND THE UPHOLDER OF ALL THINGS

God is a great mystery. A mystery is a story. A story that can be clearly explained is not a mystery. However, if there is a story that cannot be clearly explained, it is a mystery. A mystery is a story that cannot be made known or explained in a complete way. God is a mystery because although God is a story in the universe, no one can explain Him or describe Him thoroughly.

God is a mystery, and this mystery is in Jesus Christ. Jesus Christ is God's mystery, God's story. Do you want to know God? You must look at Jesus. Do you want to know more concerning what God is all about? You must come and see Jesus, and then you will know. Jesus is God's story, God's mystery. God has put all the fullness of His Godhead in Christ. Christ is the embodiment of God, the depository of God, and the expression of God. Christ is not merely God, He is God's embodiment, depository, and expression. God is hidden, but Christ is expressed. God is inexplicable, but Christ is explained. If you do not understand God, who is a mystery, you only need to come and see Christ. Christ explains God, who is a mystery. Hence, Christ is God expressed, God explained, and God spoken forth.

John 1:1 says, "In the beginning was the Word." The Word is God explained and God coming forth. This is Christ. You cannot find God outside of Christ. God has put all that He is in Christ. Ephesians 1:10 says, "Unto the economy of the fullness of the times, to head up all things in Christ." God's intention is to head up all things in Christ. Today God is still proceeding with this work of heading up all things in Christ.

When I stand, is it my two legs that support my body, or is it my head that holds up my body? Those with a shallow view will say that the feet and the legs uphold the body, but actually, according to the inner life, it is the head that holds up the body. If someone were to cut off your head, your body would immediately collapse and drop to the floor. Apparently, when I stand, it is my legs that support my body, but actually it is my head that holds up my body, heading up all the members in oneness. The head heads up and holds up the entire body.

Today the universe is in a state of collapse and disarray because it does not acknowledge Christ as the Head. The United Nations is actually a group of quarreling nations because not one nation acknowledges Christ as the Head. One day all the nations of the world will become the kingdom of our Lord and of His Christ (Rev. 11:15). At that time Christ will head up all the nations as their Head in order for God to be expressed. We all must see that God needs to obtain a corporate man to be His expression, and He also needs all things to be headed up in Christ as the Head.

CHRIST WITH THE CHURCH
AS THE UNIVERSAL, GREAT MAN

This corporate man is the Body, and Christ is the Head. Christ and this corporate man together form a universal, great man. The Head of this universal man is Christ, and the Body is the church. This universal man is God's full manifestation, God's full expression. This is God's eternal plan, God's eternal purpose.

We need to see that this is our destiny. Our destiny is not to make a fortune, to have a good family, or to have longevity, but to be the members of the corporate man with Christ as the Head to express God. This is the meaning of the universe, and this is the meaning of human life.

CHAPTER TWO

CHRIST BEING ALL

Scripture Reading: Isa. 9:6; Matt. 11:27; 16:15-16; John 3:31, 35; 17:5; Acts 10:36b; Col. 1:15-19; 2:2b, 9; 3:10-11; Eph. 1:20-23

In the last message we saw God's eternal purpose. Everyone who believes in the Lord, serves Him, and follows Him needs to see God's eternal purpose. God's eternal purpose and plan is to have a universal man. If we do not have a part in this universal man, our human life is meaningless, and all that we have is vanity.

THE NEED TO SEE CHRIST

Now we want to see that everyone who follows the Lord also needs to see Christ. To see Christ is not merely to listen to a message or to read a book about Christ but to see Christ in spirit. Our inner eyes need to be opened to see what Christ is, who Christ is, and what Christ is all about. The first vision that we must see is concerning God's eternal plan and that this plan is for Christ. Hence, we must also see Christ. This subject is so great that the Lord Jesus said, "No one fully knows the Son except the Father" (Matt. 11:27). The Son is Christ. Only God truly knows Him, and besides God no one else knows Him in a full way, because He is too great. Thank the Lord, however, that the Father not only knows the Son but is willing to reveal the Son to us (16:17). Therefore, we all should desire and pursue to know Him. We should pray, "O Father, reveal Your Son to me. O God, reveal Your Christ to me. You know Him, and I also want to know Him." We need an inner eye and an opening in our spirit that we may see the heavenly vision. Christ is so great and so wonderful. I hope that you will do your best to understand this.

CHRIST BEING ALL

The Bible tells us that "Christ is all" (Col. 3:11). In the past I have encountered opposition to this point. Some have asked me, "Does this mean that Christ is also all the filthy things?" Some also say that this word in Colossians only says that Christ is all in the new man. I acknowledge that Christ is all in the new man. However, Malachi chapter four says that Christ is the Sun of righteousness (v. 2). Is the sun in the new man? Of course it is not. Therefore, the fact that Christ is all refers not only to the fact that Christ is every constituent and every part of the new man but also to the fact that Christ is the reality of every positive thing in the universe.

In this universe there is God. Is Christ God? Yes! In this universe there is also the devil. Is Christ the devil? No! In this universe there is light. Is Christ light? Yes! In this universe there is love. Is Christ love? Yes! We should be clear that when we say Christ is all, we refer to the reality of all the positive things and not the negative things. The human personality includes both love and hatred. Is Christ love? Yes! Is Christ hatred? No! Christ is love but not hatred. The human personality also includes both humility and pride. Christ is humility but not pride.

Furthermore, we should realize that the love we have is but a shadow and that the patience we have is also but a shadow. What is a shadow? My shadow looks just like me, but it is not substantial, and it is not the real me. I am the real me. Our love is not the substance but a shadow. The substance of our love is Christ. Even the sun is merely a shadow. Its reality is Christ.

Therefore, I will boldly tell you that Christ is all. He is God, the eternal God, the God who is without beginning and without end (John 1:1). He is the Creator (Col. 1:16). He is Jehovah, the God who has a relationship with man in life (Isa. 9:6). He is God the Father as the source of everything. He was incarnated as Jesus. Hence, He is our Redeemer and Savior. Not only so, He is God expressed as the Son. He also resurrected from the dead and became the life-giving Spirit (1 Cor. 15:45b). Hence, He is the Spirit (2 Cor. 3:17). Furthermore, today He is a perfect, transcendent, and resurrected man. He is also light, life, power, authority, righteousness, and holiness. All the fullness of the Godhead dwells in Him bodily (Col. 2:9). He is all of man's virtues, such as love, patience, and humility. He is wisdom and knowledge. He is all.

All the positive things in the universe are symbols of Christ. He is the reality of the sun, the stars, and the trees on earth. In the Bible many trees symbolize Christ. He is the tree of life and the true vine. He is also the reality of the flowers. The Bible shows us that He is symbolized by different kinds of flowers. Moreover, He is the real fruit and the real grain. He is the wheat and the barley. The Gospel of John says that He is the bread (6:48) and the living water (4:14). It also says that He is the door (10:9) and the way (14:6). In the Bible there is both an entrance and an exit. Christ as the door is not only for us to go in but also for us to go out. In John 10 the Lord said, "I am the door; if anyone enters through Me, he shall...go in and go out and shall find pasture" (v. 9). The door here is not the door to heaven but the door of the sheepfold. The sheepfold is the old covenant that God made with Israel. During the dark night, the sheep are kept in the fold. Moses, David, Isaiah, and many other prophets all entered into the fold through this door. When the Lord Jesus came, Peter, James, and Paul were in there as well. They were like sheep in a fold. However, the Lord Jesus as the door provided a way for them to come out. According to the record in John 9, one of the first ones to leave the fold was the blind man. The blind man did not leave on his own but was cast out by others. At the same time, it was the Lord Jesus who led him out of the fold, since He is not only the door of the sheep but also the Shepherd. We may even say that the reality of the clothes we wear is Christ. Christ is all.

CHRIST BEING THE UNLIMITED ONE

Because Christ is all, the revelation in the Bible concerning Him is unlimited. Ephesians chapter three reveals that even the dimensions of the universe—the breadth, the length, the height, and the depth—are Christ (v. 18). No one can tell how wide the universe is. The breadth of the universe is immeasurable and boundless. The length and height of the universe are also boundless. Today, due to scientific advancements, man is able to go to the moon. According to the human perception, the distance from the earth to the moon is quite far. However, from the perspective of the whole universe, that distance is quite insignificant. The breadth, length, height, and depth of the universe are immeasurable, and all of these dimensions are Christ. Christ is the breadth, length, height, and depth of the universe. Ephesians chapter three says that when Christ makes His home in our entire being, we will know what are the breadth, length, height, and depth. Do not think that our mentality can ever thoroughly apprehend Christ. In his old age Paul wrote in Philippians 3 that he wanted to "know" Christ (v. 10a). Paul knew Christ much more than we do, yet at that time he still wanted to know more of Christ. Our Lord is all, and He is unlimited.

THE SON BEING THE FATHER, AND THE SON ALSO BEING THE SPIRIT

Because of man's limited mentality, there have been many debates and different interpretations concerning the person of Christ. In the last twenty years, in speaking concerning the experience of life, I often have spoken of the Lord Jesus being the Father, the Son, and the Spirit, and I have met opposition because of what I have said. Someone once attacked me, saying, "How can you say that the Lord Jesus is the Son and also the Father? How can you say that He is the Son and also the Spirit?" When I met this opposer ten years ago, I asked him, "If the Father is not the Son, and if the Son is not the Spirit, how can you say that God is triune? Do you have one God or three Gods?" To my surprise he answered, "I have three Gods." Immediately I warned him, saying, "You must by no means teach this kind of doctrine. To say that there are three Gods is heresy." This incident shows us that if a person has not seen that Christ is all, he will oppose this concept and say that Christ is only the Son and not the Father or the Spirit. If this were the case, then Christ would not be all. Today, however, we see that in this universe there is the Father, the Son, and the Spirit and that the Lord Jesus is the Father, the Son, and the Spirit (Isa. 9:6; 1 Cor. 15:45b; 2 Cor. 3:17). In this universe there is both God and man. The Lord Jesus is both God and man. In this universe there is the Creator and there are the creatures. Our Lord Jesus is not only the Creator but also a creature (Col. 1:15-16). Concerning this matter, another one also opposed me, saying, "To say that Christ is the Firstborn of all creation is to make Christ a creature, and this is heresy! Christ is the Creator but not a creature!" I refuted his argument by showing him that Christ became a man with bones, flesh, and blood, so He was surely a man. Was man created or not? Yes, man was created. Christ is God the Creator, yet He became a man, a created one. If you do not confess that the Lord is a creature, this means that you do not confess that He is a man. If you confess that the Lord Jesus is a man, then since man is a creature, you must confess that He is both a creature and the Creator. He is both man and God. Our Christ is all.

When you breathe, you should say, "O Lord, You are my real air." When you go down some stairs, you should say, "O Lord, You are my stairs." When you see a door, you should say, "O Lord Jesus, You are my door." When you see a window, you should say, "O Lord Jesus, You are my window for fresh air." The Scriptures clearly say that the Lord Jesus is all. Not only is He all, but He is also "Lord of all" (Acts 10:36b). *All* comprises all persons, matters, and things. He is the Lord of all persons, matters, and things.

CHRIST FILLING ALL

Furthermore, Ephesians 1:22b-23 says that the church is "the fullness of the One who fills all in all." What does this mean? We must realize that the fullness here is not Christ but the church. We must not apply the fullness here to Christ but to the church. The fullness is the church. Today in Taiwan there is so much rich produce—different kinds of grains, fruits, and vegetables, plus chickens, ducks, and other kinds of meat. These are the riches, not the fullness, of Taiwan. When we take in all these riches as our nourishment, eventually all of us will look healthy and strong. Then we may say that we are the fullness of Taiwan. Similarly, Christ is rich. When we enjoy and assimilate His riches so that they become us, we become the fullness of Christ. We are not the riches of Christ but the fullness of Christ. The riches of Christ are all that Christ is, and when all these riches become us, we become His fullness.

Let us come back to the matter of Christ being all. Do you see that Christ is all? Is Christ the reality of the heavens? Yes! Is Christ the reality of the earth? Yes! The emergence of the dry land from the death waters on the third day in Genesis 1 is a type of Christ who resurrected from the dead. Christ is typified not only by the light and the expanse but also by the land, which was raised out of the death waters on the third day. In the same chapter you see that the plants, animals, and mankind all came out of the earth. This signifies that life comes out of the resurrected Christ. Furthermore, the land of Canaan promised by God to His chosen people is a type of the Lord Jesus. The land of Canaan is surrounded by water—the Mediterranean Sea, the Dead Sea, and the Jordan River. This land, which is two to three thousand feet above sea level, is a type of Christ as the resurrected, transcendent One and as the source of life. Hence, we may say that Christ is the real land.

If people had such an enlarged view of Christ as all, then they would not argue, saying that Christ is the Son but not the Father. They would not say that Christ is the Creator but not a creature. The Bible says that Christ is the Lamb and the Lion. Is a lion the Creator or a creature? It is true that the Bible says that Christ is the Creator, in whom all things were created (Col. 1:16). However, Christ also became a created one. He became the Lamb, the Lion, and a vine. Are these items created things or the Creator? If we had a complete view and saw that Christ is all, then we would not argue. Hallelujah! Christ is indeed all!

CHRIST BECOMING US AND WE BECOMING CHRIST

Finally, since Christ is all, Christ must be the real me. Let me ask you, "Is Christ you?" You must say, "Yes, Christ is me because Christ is all, and I am included in all!" I am not something negative. As a human being, I am something positive, so Christ is surely the real me. Thank and praise the Lord that Christ is the real us! In Him we see God, and in Him we also see ourselves! Do you have the boldness to say that Christ is the real you? The last two lines of stanza 4 of Hymn #130 in the Chinese hymnal say, "Thou became me, and I became Thee: / 'Tis Thy love to the uttermost!" Since the first part of that line says, "Thou became me," it naturally follows that the second part should say, "I became Thee." Some have opposed this, saying, "To say that Christ became us may be all right because Christ became flesh. However, if we say that we have become Christ, that means that we have become God. Is this not blasphemy?" I do not know what kind of mind those opposing people have. Would it not be ridiculous for someone to say that four plus four equals eight but that eight does not equal four plus four? The Bible says that we are members of the Body of Christ. Suppose I said, "This arm is a member of this brother, but it is not this brother himself. Therefore, when I hit this member, I am not hitting this brother himself." This kind of logic does not make any sense. We have all become members of Christ, so how can we not be Christ? Not only so, 1 Corinthians 12 says explicitly that the Body is Christ: "For even as the body is one and has many members, yet all the members of the body, being many, are one body, so also is the Christ" (v. 12). *The Christ* here is the Body. Therefore, to say "Thou became me, and I became Thee" is not heresy. Furthermore, the Lord Jesus said that He is the vine and that we are the branches (John 15:5). The branches are included in the vine. We may even say that the branches are the vine.

This is the wonder of wonders and the mystery of mysteries—that Christ is all. If we all would know Christ to such an extent, how noble we would be! Christ is me, and I am Christ! He is Christ in me. Is God in the Bible? Then who is God? God is Christ. Is Jehovah in the Scriptures? Then who is Jehovah? Jehovah is Christ. Is the Father in the Bible? Then who is the Father? The Father is Christ (Isa. 9:6). Is the Son in the Scriptures? Then who is the Son? The Son is Christ! Is the Spirit in the Bible? Then who is the Spirit? The Spirit is Christ (1 Cor. 15:45b). Is man in the Scriptures? Then who is the real man? The real man is Christ. Are you in the Bible? Then who is the real you? The real you is Christ! Hallelujah! Christ is all. Christ is not only all in the new man but also all in the whole universe.

We must see that Christ is our life, our virtues, and our all in all. Where is He? He is in our spirit. What is He in our spirit? He is the Spirit in our spirit. This Christ who has become our all is in our spirit as the all-inclusive, life-giving Spirit. Today, we live by Christ when we live by the Spirit. When we live by Him, we allow Him to live Himself through us. When He lives Himself out of us, then it is possible for us to live Christ.

If we seek the Lord, sooner or later He will open our eyes to see that as the Christ of all, He is all. He is not only the Father, the Son, and the Spirit, He is also the reality of all positive things. Hallelujah! We must see the all-inclusive Christ. The greatest mystery in the universe is that He can become us and we can become Him. As the all-inclusive Spirit He enters into our regenerated spirit to be joined and mingled with us. The two spirits—His Spirit and our spirit—became one spirit (1 Cor. 6:17). He lives instead of us, and we live by Him (Gal. 2:20). Therefore, what we live out is Christ. For to us, to live is Christ (Phil. 1:21).

CHAPTER THREE

THE CHURCH AS THE NEW MAN

Scripture Reading: Matt. 16:18-19; Eph. 1:22-23; 2:15-16, 21-22; 3:4-6; 4:4-6, 22-24; 5:25-27, 32; 1 Tim. 3:15-16; Rev. 1:11

CHRIST BEING THE SPIRIT

In the previous messages we stated that we must see God's eternal purpose and that we must also see Christ. The term *Christ* has become too common among people today. Today the whole world knows this term, yet very few truly know Christ. Although we may know the Bible very well, we may not have a thorough and real knowledge of Christ. We should not have merely an empty vision of the knowledge of Christ. We need to have a practical knowledge of Christ.

One time someone sincerely advised me, saying, "Do not teach anymore that Christ is the Spirit, because those in Christianity cannot understand it and do not approve of it. They consider the Father, the Son, and the Holy Spirit to be three separate Persons. They think that the Father is high above in the heavens and that the Son came to the earth, died, resurrected, ascended to the throne, and is now sitting at the right hand of the Father. They believe that the Father and the Son are two separate Persons. Therefore, you must not say that the Son is the Father. Above all, you must not say that the Son is the Spirit. Do not say that Christ is the life-giving Spirit."

If this were merely a matter of doctrine, I would not speak so much about it. However, the Lord is advancing in His recovery today, and the most important item in His recovery is the mingling of God with man. Today Christ is actually dwelling in us. Those in Christianity may ask, "If Christ is sitting in the heavens, how can He dwell in us at the same time? What is your scriptural basis for saying this?" Our basis for saying this is Colossians 1:27, which says that Christ is in us as the hope of glory. At the same time, however, the Bible also says that Christ is in the heavens. Therefore, in order to see that Christ is the Spirit, we must speak from the perspective of experience. If you speak according to empty doctrines, you may end up separating God into three separate Persons. However, if you consider your actual experience, you will discover that Christ is the Spirit. In my youth I was under the influence of traditional teachings. However, when I became serious and began to seek the Lord, I found out that although on the surface many of these teachings seem to be right, they do not agree with our experience. According to our experience, Christ is in us. The Bible clearly shows us that as the source, Christ is the Father, and as the One who enters into us, He is the Spirit.

Isaiah 9:6 says, on the one hand, that He is a child and a son, and on the other hand, that He is the mighty God and the eternal Father. Some people, however, only believe that the child born in the manger was the mighty God. They do not believe that the Son who was manifested is the eternal Father. Another verse, 2 Corinthians 3:17, says, "The Lord is the Spirit." If you show these two verses to the opposers, they will have nothing to say. They will eventually have to admit that they do not understand this matter. If we cannot even understand man, who is so small, how can we comprehend the Triune God, who is so great? For decades I was cheated by Christianity and was kept ignorant, until one day I decided that I did not want to be ignorant any longer. I did not try to understand the truth in the Bible. I simply accepted it. The Bible says, "A son is given to us...and His name will be called...Eternal Father" (Isa. 9:6). The Bible also says that the Lord is the Spirit (2 Cor. 3:17). I must accept these words whether I understand them or not, because they are in the Bible. My understanding may be wrong, but the Bible cannot be wrong.

When Saul of Tarsus was on the road to Damascus, the Lord Jesus suddenly appeared to him, saying, "Saul, Saul, why are you persecuting Me?" (Acts 9:4). Saul must have been thinking, "I persecuted Stephen, Peter, James, and John. They are all people on the earth. I never persecuted anyone in the heavens. Yet this voice that is coming from the heavens is saying, 'Why are you persecuting Me?' Who could this be?" He did not understand what this was all about, so he asked, "Who are You, Lord?" The Lord then said, "I am Jesus, whom you persecute" (v. 5). Then Saul saw a vision—the vision of the Body of Christ. He saw that when he had been persecuting Stephen, he had been persecuting Christ, because Stephen was a part of Christ. Stephen had become Christ. On the day of his conversion, Saul of Tarsus was opened by the Lord to see that the church is the Body of Christ. Jesus is no longer the individual Jesus. Today He is in the heavens and also on the earth because He has become us and we have become Him.

Perhaps someone will ask, "If a Christian goes to the movies, plays mah-jongg, beats people, and commits arson, is that person also Christ?" Of course, that kind of living is of the devil and not of Christ. That is the devil in the flesh. When we say that we Christians are Christ, we are referring to the Christ in our spirit. When we live by the spirit, we are Christ. We do not mean that we have become God in His Godhead. Rather, what we mean is that we are the same as Christ is in life and nature. Praise Him! He has God's life, and we also have God's life. He has God's nature, and we also have God's nature.

Furthermore, this all-inclusive Christ, who is all, is in us. We must see such a light. We need to know such a Christ. He is so small that He can come into us, yet He is so great that the universe cannot contain Him. He is the One who fills all in all. He is so great. Moreover, all that God is and has are in Him. Apart from Christ we cannot find God. Christ is God's story, God's mystery. Christ is too marvelous!

THE CHURCH BEING THE NEW MAN

If you know Christ, then you must also know the church. Matthew chapter sixteen shows us that if you know Christ, you need to also know the church. Peter said to the Lord, "You are the Christ, the Son of the living God" (v. 16). Then the Lord answered him, "I also say to you...upon this rock I will build My church" (v. 18). Then, after mentioning the church, He went on to speak concerning the kingdom of the heavens. The kingdom of the heavens is the church, and the church is the kingdom of the heavens. We should pray-read all the verses concerning the church in the first five chapters of Ephesians. What is revealed in these chapters is not a natural thought or a human concept but a divine revelation. The church is not only the Body but also the new man. Formerly every one of us was an old man, but today, having been saved, we are all in the church, and every one of us is a new man.

In order for a person to have a part in the church, he must see that his old man was terminated on the cross. Everyone who comes into the church needs to first leave his old man on the cross. This teaching is clear, and in theory it sounds very good. However, after a long period of practicing this, we still may be unable to leave our old man on the cross. Even if we are able, it may be only temporary. This is not because the teaching that the old man should be terminated is wrong. When we come to Ephesians 4, we see that merely crucifying the old man is not enough. The old man also needs to be put off. What we need is not just a short-term crucifying of the old man but a long-term putting off of the old man.

PUTTING OFF THE OLD MAN AND
PUTTING ON THE NEW MAN

Now we must see what the new man is. The new man is Christ as the Spirit, the life-giving Spirit, and the all-inclusive Spirit. This Spirit is Christ (2 Cor. 3:17). When you believe in Christ, the Spirit enters into you. However, do not think that now we have only the new man. We must realize that now we have two men. On the outside is the old man, and on the inside is the new man. To use the utterance of the Scriptures, our spirit as our inner man is the new man, and our flesh as our outer being is the old man. If someone scolded you and you became very angry, you would be expressing the old man. Thank the Lord that we are a new man, not in our flesh but in our spirit. However, we need to remember that we have the old man as well as the new man. This is why in Ephesians chapter four Paul says that we need to put off the old man (v. 22). If someone scolds us, we should not get angry. Instead, we should quickly put off our old man. The more we are rebuked, the more we should put off the old man. If we do this, eventually we will even be able to help them with the rebuking. We must lay aside our old man and should by no means put on the old man.

We also need to be renewed in the spirit of our mind (v. 23). Those who have been completely renewed in the spirit of their mind can completely ignore everything of the old man. Their concepts have been changed completely. This is not an easy matter. We should not say that we have already heard this teaching, because merely hearing this teaching is useless. If a person loves the Lord very much, yet he often vindicates himself or holds a grudge when he is wronged by others, then he has not put off the old man. If you still have a grievance and cannot let go of it, this proves that you are still putting on the old man. If you have put off the old man, you will realize that regardless of how others have offended you, they have offended your old man and not your new man. Your new man is in another realm. Therefore, we need to change our concept altogether by being renewed in the spirit of our mind. Then, when others offend us, we will no longer become angry, nor will we feel offended, because the one who was offended was our old man. Even if they were able to cut up our old man into many pieces and then bury or burn the pieces, we would not feel anything because we have put off our old man. This is easy to say but very difficult to experience. The one way we can experience this is by turning to our spirit. There is a new man within us. We need to turn to our spirit because there is indeed a new man within us.

This new man is the church. To put on the new man is to put on the church, and to put on the new man is to live the church life. If you do not know the church to this extent, you may be very burning today, but tomorrow you will cool down. If you know the church, you will put off the old man and put on the new. I do not care how others treat me because ultimately they help me to put off the old man. We should not view our relationships with one another according to our natural perception. Instead, we should view them altogether in the new man. Gradually, the brother who offended you will also see the light. When he sees that, instead of being offended, you have put on the new man, he will also give up his natural being and put on the new man. In this way your coordination in the church will be in oneness, the genuine oneness that cannot be broken.

We must realize that the church is the new man. If we truly see that the church is the new man, and if we put off the old man and put on the new, we will never be a problem in the church. If this is the case, we will spontaneously stand on the ground of the church, and there will definitely be the oneness. This is possible because the Body is one and the Spirit is also one. When we are in spirit, we are on the ground of oneness. As long as we are in spirit, we are in the oneness. We need to see the church, which is very mysterious. According to experience, the church is the golden lampstand, and the golden lampstand is the seven Spirits. The seven Spirits should be the church life today. To be the church is to live under the control of the seven Spirits and to continually walk in the spirit. We need to know God's eternal purpose, we need to know Christ, and even more, we need to know the church. Christ is all, and the church is in the Spirit. Christ is all, and the church is the new man. Therefore, every day we need to learn this basic lesson of turning to the spirit, putting off the old man, and putting on the new man.

NOT NEEDING HELP FROM THE CIRCUMSTANCES BUT NEEDING TO TURN TO OUR SPIRIT

We do not need the brothers and sisters to help us put off the old man. Ephesians only says that we should put off the old man and put on the new man. When we helped others in the past, we may not have been absolutely pure to the extent that the element of Christianity had been completely purged out of us. Sometimes the help we render to people can change in nature without our realizing it. I used to say that our wives and our children help us to be dealt with. Today, however, I hope we can see that we do not necessarily need these ones.

The reason why these ones are often necessary is because we often force the Lord to the point where He has no alternative but to use these ones to help us. Let us use the disciplining of students as an illustration. Most students do not need to be disciplined every day. A student who does not study unless he is disciplined is a bad student. A good student or a good child does not need discipline.

We need to see that because Ephesians speaks from the heavens, there is no need for help from the circumstances on the earth. In Ephesians the shining, enlightenment, and revelation all come from the heavens. Thus, there is little need for earthly help. God's grace is so sufficient that there is no need to have a great deal of outward help from the circumstances. If we need such help, it is because of our weakness and dullness. Therefore, we must not receive the words concerning being broken and being dealt with according to our natural concept. Such words are usually received in a way that is too natural. Whether or not you have a wife, and whether or not you have the circumstances, you need to always put off the old man and put on the new.

To put on the new man is to turn to our spirit. It does not matter how the brothers and sisters treat us. We simply need to turn to our spirit. Then we will not need the help from the outward circumstances because we will be constantly turning to our spirit. The church is the new man, and this new man is in our spirit.

Because we have not clearly seen this positive vision nor sufficiently received this positive light, there have been many teachings, even among us, that lean toward the natural concept. It is easy for people to agree with teachings that lean toward the natural concept, but it is not so easy for them to accept a teaching that has been purely released from the heavens as light or a vision. Today we must realize that we do not necessarily need the outward circumstances. All that matters is that we put off the old man, put on the new, and live in our spirit.

On the day of Pentecost when Peter stood up to give a message, he was completely beside himself. Later, after healing the lame man, he spoke to the people at the portico called

Solomon's, saying, "Men of Israel,...you denied the holy and righteous One;...and the Author of life you killed..." (Acts 3:11-15). If I had been there on that day, I would not have let Peter go. I would have interrupted him right on the spot, saying, "Peter, do you remember what you did a few weeks ago? You denied the Lord three times in one night, and now you still have the audacity to speak?" Peter stood there that day to speak as if nothing had happened, as if he had not failed before. How could he do that? He could do that because he had put on the new man. He had put off the Peter who had rejected the Lord and had put on the new man. Everything is all right when we turn to our spirit. We are not a civic organization discussing character cultivation and behavior improvement. We need to turn to our spirit and live in our spirit. We must look to the Lord that the churches would not remain old but would remove all the oldness and become altogether new.

CHAPTER FOUR

THE SEVEN SPIRITS OF GOD AND OUR SPIRIT

THE CHURCH AS THE NEW MAN BEING ALTOGETHER A MATTER IN SPIRIT

We must see that the church is the new man. In the past we clearly pointed out that the church is the Body. However, we were not so clear that the church is the new man. It was not until recently that the Lord clearly showed us that the church is not only the Body but also the new man.

Why are we pointing out this matter? We are pointing out this matter because when we read the Bible, it is not easy to find verses linking the church as the Body to the Spirit. The best verse one can find is Ephesians 4:4a, which says, "One Body and one Spirit." From this verse, it seems that the Spirit and the Body are linked. It is also possible to see this in 1 Corinthians 12:13a, which says, "For also in one Spirit we were all baptized into one Body." In this verse we may also see a link, although this verse is not directly about the church but about Christ, because verse 12 explicitly says that the Body is Christ. In the past we said numerous times that Christ is not only the Head but also the Body. Christ is the church, and the church is Christ, because the church is the Body of Christ. However, we did not point out clearly enough that the church is the new man. In speaking of the Body, the emphasis is mostly on Christ. In speaking of the new man, the emphasis is altogether on the Spirit.

What is the church? The church is the new man. Where is the new man? The new man is in our spirit. In the past we heard many messages on the cross, on being broken, and on being dealt with. We were told that God deals with us through our wives, our husbands, our children, illnesses, and all kinds of adverse situations. There was nothing wrong with those messages, but there was a great lack in them. It is possible to be dealt with yet not be in the spirit. It is possible to be broken yet still not be in the spirit. Only in the spirit can there be the new man. The new man is the Spirit and is in our spirit. The Spirit in the new man is the all-inclusive, life-giving Spirit, who is the Lord Himself who went through death and resurrection. This life-giving Spirit in our spirit becomes the corporate new man. Therefore, the Lord is bringing us, step by step, from the Body to the new man.

Ten years ago we saw that the church is the new man, but we did not see it clearly enough, and it did not become a burden in us. I can testify that when I was releasing messages fifteen years ago, every time I spoke about the church, my burden was mainly on the church as the Body. However, today when I speak concerning the church, my inner burden is on the church as the new man. The new man is the all-inclusive Spirit in our spirit. The genuine church life is not merely a matter of receiving the cross, being dealt with, and being broken on the negative side, but a matter of touching the spirit on the positive side. It is not because we have been broken that there is the church. It is not because we have been dealt with that there is the church. It is not because we have been crucified on the cross that there is the church. No! Only when our spirit is released can there be the church. This is because the church as the new man is in our spirit. Therefore, we must turn to our spirit.

If we all could see this light and have a sufficiently clear vision concerning this matter, then we would not need to be dealt with so much by God, because by living in our spirit we would spontaneously put off our old man and put on the new man every day. Consider your experience. Is it not true that when you are truly in spirit, your old man is put off? Every time we are in spirit, we put off our old man and put on the new man. Once we put on the new man, the church becomes something practical to us—the church life. The church life is the living of the new man. How can we have such a living? We spontaneously put on such a living when we turn to our spirit. Once we turn to our spirit, we put off the old man and put on the new man.

NOT EMPHASIZING INDIVIDUAL SPIRITUALITY BUT PUTTING ON THE NEW MAN IN SPIRIT

From accounts of church history and numerous biographies, we can see that those who received the cross, the breaking, and the dealing might have gained a certain measure of spiritual edification for themselves, but they did not necessarily have the church life. Moreover, most of those who spoke concerning the cross, the breaking, and the dealing did not emphasize the church. Rather, they emphasized only individual spirituality. What God wants today, however, is not spiritual individuals. Instead, He wants the church life. We need to live in the spirit and put on the new man, because the new man is the church life. This is genuine spirituality. Our spirituality must be tested by the church. Any spirituality that cannot stand the test of the church is not genuine. Rather, it is a false spirituality, a questionable spirituality.

I have seen many people who were quite spiritual, but every one of them was individualistic. I ask you to consider whether the spiritual ones that you admired from the past to the present were individualistic or not. It seems that the more spiritual people are, the more individualistic they become. They become so spiritual that they cannot respect anyone else. They do not admire anyone except themselves. Those who are individually spiritual have little respect for others. Consequently, they cannot get along with others. I do not believe that we have ever seen two spiritual persons cooperating with each other. This is because in the past those who spoke about the breaking of the cross and the dealings through the circumstances overemphasized individual spirituality. In their sermons they rarely mentioned that the breaking is for the church.

However, what the Lord is showing us today is that we should live in spirit and not emphasize individual spirituality. To live in spirit is to put on the church life. Whether or not we are spiritual, whether or not we are broken, whether or not we are under the dealing of the cross, or whether or not we are going through circumstances, we simply need to put on the new man to reach God's goal. The new man is not individual but corporate, having been created with two peoples—the Jews and the Gentiles. You cannot find the new man in either the breaking of the cross or in the dealings of the circumstances. You can find the new man only in the spirit. You need only to be in the spirit. Then the old man is put off and the new man is put on. When you are in the spirit, you cannot be individualistic, and you also cannot help going to the church meetings and seeking out the brothers and sisters.

In the following sections we will study the Bible. In these days the Lord has given us fresh light in His Word. Therefore, we need to study the Word carefully.

THE STONE WITH SEVEN EYES

Let us first read Zechariah chapter three. Verse 9, which is a wonderful Bible verse, says, "For here is the stone that I have set before Joshua—upon one stone are seven eyes." This is very interesting. Have you ever seen a stone with seven eyes? What does this mean? Suppose there is a piece of stone here that grows eyes that can see you. Such a piece of stone must be living. Therefore, the stone with eyes in this verse is a living stone. It is very interesting that the Bible does not put the word *living* in the record, yet we are able to discover it in our reading. How do we know that this stone is living? We know because it has eyes. It not only has eyes, it has seven eyes. In the Bible the number seven means completion intensified. This stone is not only living, but its livingness is sevenfold intensified.

There is a stone, and upon it are seven eyes. Who is this stone? The verse continues, saying, "I will engrave its engraving, declares Jehovah of hosts, and I will remove the iniquity of that land in one day." This stone in God's dealing hand is a stone that removes iniquities. The iniquities of God's people were removed in one day. Who is this stone? "Behold, the Lamb of God, who takes away the sin of the world!" (John 1:29). This stone is the Lamb of God. Another verse that proves that this stone is the Lamb of God is Revelation 5:6. This verse says, "And I saw in the midst of the throne and of

the four living creatures and in the midst of the elders a
Lamb standing as having just been slain, having seven horns
and seven eyes, which are the seven Spirits of God." The
Lamb has seven eyes. Therefore, the stone with seven eyes in
Zechariah 3 is the Lamb with seven eyes in Revelation 5. The
Lamb is Christ. Hence, this stone is Christ. Christ is living,
Christ redeemed us from our sins, and Christ has seven eyes.
Since Christ is something living and something for
redemption, why is He a stone? This stone is for the building.
Matthew 21:42 says, "Jesus said to them, Have you never read
in the Scriptures, 'The stone which the builders rejected, this
has become the head of the corner. This was from the Lord,
and it is marvelous in our eyes'?" The stone that the builders
rejected is for the building as indicated by the builders' original intention to use it.

Acts 4:12 says, "And there is salvation in no other, for neither
is there another name under heaven given among men in which
we must be saved." According to verse 11, this means that
there is salvation in no one except the stone rejected by the
builders. Those in Christianity often quote Acts 4:12 but ignore
4:11. This is because most Christian preachers preach salvation but not building. They preach about the Redeemer but
not about the stone. Therefore, recently I released several
messages telling people that our Savior is the Stone-Savior.
Our Savior is a stone, and this stone is a living stone and a
redeeming stone. He saves us not to bring us to heaven but to
transform us, who are sinners made of clay, into stones with
His stony nature and element. He is not bringing us to heaven.
He is building us into the New Jerusalem. Hallelujah!

Ephesians 2:20-22 says, "Being built upon the foundation
of the apostles and prophets, Christ Jesus Himself being the
cornerstone; in whom all the building, being fitted together, is
growing into a holy temple in the Lord; in whom you also are
being built together into a dwelling place of God in spirit."
The Lord Jesus has become the cornerstone for the building
of the church.

First Peter 2:4-5 says, "Coming to Him, a living stone,
rejected by men but with God chosen and precious, you yourselves also, as living stones, are being built up as a spiritual

house into a holy priesthood to offer up spiritual sacrifices acceptable to God through Jesus Christ." This passage clearly says that the Lord is the stone.

SEVEN EYES, SEVEN LAMPS, AND SEVEN SPIRITS

Now we must find out what the seven eyes are. Zechariah 4:2 says, "And he said to me, What do you see? And I said, I see that there is a lampstand all of gold, with its bowl on top of it and its seven lamps upon it." Chapter three says that "upon one stone are seven eyes" (v. 9). Chapter four says that upon the lampstand are seven lamps. Can we say that the stone in chapter three is the lampstand in chapter four? Can we say that the seven eyes in chapter three are the seven lamps in chapter four? Yes, we can! We can say this because verse 10 of chapter four says, "For who has despised the day of small things? For these seven...." I believe that *these seven* refers not to the seven eyes but to the seven lamps, because chapter four mentions the seven lamps in verse 2 and then explains the meaning of these words in verse 10. *These seven* refers to the seven lamps. "They are the eyes of Jehovah." Do you see this? The seven eyes upon the stone are the eyes of Jehovah. How could the seven eyes of Jehovah be upon the stone? This study of the Bible is truly wonderful. After reading the Bible again and again, we have discovered that the eyes of Jehovah are the seven eyes on the stone and that the seven eyes on the stone are the seven lamps on the lampstand.

The seven lamps in chapter four are, without a doubt, the seven eyes of God. These seven eyes cannot be another seven eyes in addition to the seven eyes in chapter three. The seven eyes in chapter three are the seven eyes on the stone, and the seven eyes in chapter four are the seven eyes of Jehovah. Therefore, this implies that the seven eyes of Jehovah are upon the stone. Who is the stone? The stone is Jehovah! The stone is Jesus, and the name Jesus means "Jehovah the Savior." Thus, the seven eyes on the stone are the seven eyes of Jehovah because the stone is Jehovah. The stone is Jesus, who is Jehovah—the redeeming Jehovah, Jehovah who removes our iniquities, Jehovah as our Savior, and Jehovah as the Lamb of God. Therefore, His seven eyes are God's seven eyes.

In Zechariah chapters three and four there are the seven eyes on the stone, the seven lamps on the lampstand, and the seven eyes of Jehovah. These verses show us that the seven eyes on the stone are the seven lamps on the lampstand, and the seven lamps on the lampstand are the seven eyes of Jehovah. Hence, these three refer to the same thing. The seven eyes on the stone, the seven lamps on the lampstand, and the eyes of Jehovah all speak of the same thing. What is this thing? The answer is in Zechariah.

Zechariah 4:4 says, "And I answered and spoke to the angel who spoke with me, saying, What are these, sir?" What is the significance of the one lampstand with seven lamps? Verses 5 and 6 say, "And the angel who spoke with me answered and said to me, Do you not know what these are? And I said, No, sir. And he answered and spoke to me, saying, This is the word of Jehovah to Zerubbabel, saying, Not by might nor by power, but by My Spirit, says Jehovah of hosts." This clearly indicates that the one lampstand with seven lamps is "My Spirit." In other words, the lampstand with seven lamps is the Spirit of God.

Verse 7 says, "Who are you, O great mountain? Before Zerubbabel you will become a plain, and he will bring forth the topstone with shouts of Grace, grace to it." The topstone is the stone on the top of a house. This topstone is the stone with seven eyes in chapter three. Verses 8 to 10 say, "Moreover the word of Jehovah came to me, saying, The hands of Zerubbabel have laid the foundation of this house, and his hands will finish it; and you will know that Jehovah of hosts has sent Me to you. For who has despised the day of small things? For these seven rejoice when they see the plummet in the hand of Zerubbabel; they are the eyes of Jehovah running to and fro on the whole earth." The plummet in the hand is for building. Hence, all these items are for the building of God's temple. The stone having seven eyes, the lampstand having seven lamps, and the eyes of Jehovah are just one entity. This entity is the Spirit of Jehovah. In brief, the seven eyes are the seven Spirits of God for His building.

Now let us come to Revelation. Revelation 4:5b says, "There were seven lamps of fire burning before the throne, which are the seven Spirits of God." This verse clearly says that the seven lamps are the seven Spirits of God. Let us also read 5:6, which says, "And I saw in the midst of the throne and of the four living creatures and in the midst of the elders a Lamb standing as having just been slain, having seven horns and seven eyes, which are the seven Spirits of God." The seven lamps are the seven Spirits of God, and the seven eyes are also the seven Spirits of God. Where did the seven lamps in Revelation come from? They came from Zechariah. Where did the seven eyes in Revelation come from? They also came from Zechariah. Zechariah mentions seven eyes, and Revelation also speaks of seven eyes. Zechariah mentions seven lamps, and Revelation also speaks of seven lamps. Furthermore, in Revelation we are clearly told that the seven eyes are the seven lamps. This indicates that the seven eyes upon the stone in Zechariah 3 are the seven lamps on the lampstand. Hence, the seven eyes are the seven Spirits of God, and the seven lamps are also the seven Spirits of God. The seven eyes and the seven lamps both signify the seven Spirits of God. This absolutely corresponds with what was written in Zechariah 4:4-6. In these verses Zechariah asked, "What are these, sir?" and the angel replied that they were the Spirit of Jehovah.

THE LAMPSTAND BEING
BOTH CHRIST AND THE SPIRIT

These verses show us that the lampstand in Zechariah 4 signifies the Spirit. In the Old Testament two lampstands are mentioned. One of them was in the tabernacle and later in the temple. The lampstand in the Holy Place within the tabernacle was also a lampstand with seven lamps. In typology, that lampstand denotes Christ. However, in Zechariah 4 there is another lampstand, and that lampstand denotes the Spirit. The lampstand in the tabernacle denotes Christ, whereas the lampstand in Zechariah 4 denotes the Spirit. Since both lampstands are the same, why is it that one signifies Christ and the other signifies the Spirit? This is because the two are actually one. That which is in the Holy Place is Christ, and that which has come to the earth is the Spirit. The lampstand in the Holy Place is Christ, and the lampstand that came to the earth for the building of God is the Spirit. The one in heaven is Christ, and the one that has come to us is the Spirit. The two are one.

How do we know that the lampstand is both the Spirit and Christ? We know this because Zechariah 4 says that there is a lampstand with seven lamps, while chapter three says that there is a stone with seven eyes. The seven eyes on the stone are the seven lamps on the lampstand. Thus, the stone must be equal to the lampstand. This indicates that Christ, who took away our iniquities, became the life-giving Spirit (1 Cor. 15:45b). In Zechariah 3 He takes away our iniquities, and in chapter four He has become the life-giving Spirit. When He went to the heavens, He was Christ, and when He comes to us, He is the Spirit.

THE CHURCH LIFE DEPENDING UPON OUR RECEIVING THE WORK OF THE SEVEN SPIRITS

I have spent much time to show you that in the Lord's recovery today we should be engaged in the church life all day long. Today we are opposed for living the church life. Some have even advised me not to speak about the church. However, the more they advise me not to speak, the louder I speak. This is my burden, and this is what I speak wherever I go. In the West they call me a troublemaker, one who causes trouble. They are right. I hope to cause trouble among all the Christians, troubling them until day and night they have no peace, until the pastors can no longer function as such, and until the system can no longer continue to exist.

Do not think that I am the first troublemaker. John the Baptist and the Lord Jesus were also troublemakers. In those days when the chief priests were burning incense in the temple, they were at peace with one another, and everything was calm and peaceful. When John the Baptist and the Lord Jesus came, everywhere they went they shouted, "Brood of vipers, repent!" Both John and the Lord Jesus were troublemakers. However, in reality they did not make trouble. Instead, they brought peace with them. When the Lord troubles you,

you may feel bad at the time, but after the troubling, you will truly have peace. The church life is a peaceful life, a restful life. What God has in store for us is the rest of rests—the church life. We must enter into the church life that we may enter into such a rest.

We all need to see that Christ is not only a stone but also a lampstand. The seven lamps on the lampstand are the seven eyes on the stone. Both the seven eyes and the seven lamps signify the seven Spirits of God for transfusing and infusing the things of God into us and for shining Christ's essence into us. He not only removes our sins but also transforms us from clay into stone. This is the work of the seven Spirits. I earnestly hope that all the brothers and sisters could see this matter of the redeeming stone being a lampstand. The redeeming stone has seven eyes, and the lampstand has seven lamps. The seven eyes observe us, and the seven lamps shine over us. These are the seven Spirits of God. The Spirit's shining shines God into us, and His observing infuses Christ's essence into us, transforming us into stones good for God's building.

This is not an ethical teaching, a religious teaching, or a teaching from Christianity. This is the revelation in God's Word. We all must see this. The stone rejected by men and judged by God on the cross is the lampstand today. His seven eyes are seven lamps. When He observes you, He shines upon you. This is the work of the seven Spirits of God today. Hence, in order to have the church life and the reality of the church, the seven Spirits are indispensable. "He who has an ear, let him hear what the Spirit says to the churches" (Rev. 2:7a). "The Spirit and the bride say, Come!" (22:17a).

Today in the Lord's recovery we need to contact the seven Spirits for the Lord's churches. When we contact the seven Spirits, we contact the stone, that is, we contact Christ, and we contact God, because the seven Spirits infuse God and Christ into us. We need to allow the seven Spirits to shine upon us and to observe us. When the Spirit comes, Christ comes. When the Spirit comes, God comes. When the Spirit comes, we become stones. When the Spirit comes, we become the building materials.

OUR SPIRIT AND THE SEVEN SPIRITS OF GOD

Now let us come back to the wonderful book of Zechariah. Zechariah 12:1 says, "Thus declares Jehovah, who stretches forth the heavens and lays the foundations of the earth and forms the spirit of man within him." This is the only verse in the entire Bible that specifically indicates that God formed the spirit of man within him. This verse ranks our spirit with the heavens and the earth. Jehovah stretched forth the heavens, laid the foundations of the earth, and formed the spirit of man within him. The heavens, the earth, and the spirit are all equally ranked. Why does Zechariah mention this? Zechariah mentions this because this book speaks of God's building, which absolutely depends upon the seven Spirits of God. On God's side there is the Spirit of God, which is the seven Spirits of God, but on our side there must be our spirit. It is not sufficient simply to see the seven Spirits of God. We still need to see that we have a spirit. God has seven eyes shining upon us, and we have a spirit within us.

Zechariah 12:10 says, "I will pour out on the house of David...the Spirit of grace and of supplications." In 12:1 our spirit is mentioned, and then in verse 10 the Spirit of God is mentioned. Our spirit is like a receiving vessel, and the Spirit of God is like rain poured out. If we would read the book of Zechariah as a whole, we would see that the building of the temple typifies the building of the church today. We would see that God's building on earth depends upon the pouring out of His Spirit. Moreover, His Spirit in His building is the seven Spirits, the seven lamps, and the seven eyes. We can receive such a Spirit by the spirit within us.

Revelation 1:4 says, "John to the seven churches which are in Asia: Grace to you and peace from Him who is and who was and who is coming, and from the seven Spirits who are before His throne." Grace comes from the seven Spirits to the seven churches.

Verses 10 and 11 say, "I was in spirit on the Lord's Day and heard behind me a loud voice like a trumpet, saying, What you see write in a scroll and send it to the seven churches: to Ephesus and to Smyrna and to Pergamos and to Thyatira and to Sardis and to Philadelphia and to Laodicea." John first mentioned the seven Spirits, and then he said, "I was in spirit." Today we all must say, "O Lord, the seven Spirits are here, and we are also in our spirit." This is sufficient, and this is the church life.

**ENJOYING THE SPIRIT
TO BECOME STONES FOR BUILDING**

Revelation 2:17 says, "He who has an ear, let him hear what the Spirit says to the churches. To him who overcomes, to him I will give of the hidden manna, and to him I will give a white stone." What is this white stone? This white stone is us! When we eat the hidden manna, the element of Christ as the stone enters into us. Consequently, we become stones. Therefore, the Lord will give us a sign—a stone. This indicates that we are stones in God's eyes. He who has an ear, let him hear what the Spirit says to the churches. He who hears is an overcomer, and he who overcomes will enjoy Christ as the stone with seven eyes. The essence of the stone will get into him. You are what you eat. If you eat fish, you will smell like fish. If you eat beef, you will gradually smell like a cow. What you eat becomes you. Our eating Christ as the hidden manna is for the building, in which Christ is a stone. Christ is the manna for our eating, and He is the stone for God's building. What we take in is manna, but eventually the essence of the stone transforms us into stones. Therefore, the Lord will give us a stone, signifying that we are stones.

Revelation 3:12 begins, "He who overcomes, him I will make a pillar in the temple of My God." The overcomer is no longer just a stone, but the stone has become a pillar built into the temple of God. What is the temple of God? The temple of God is the church. "And he shall by no means go out anymore, and I will write upon him the name of My God and the name of the city of My God, the New Jerusalem, which descends out of heaven from My God, and My new name" (v. 12b). Ultimately, the church becomes the New Jerusalem.

This is the Lord's recovery today. This recovery depends on our touching the Spirit as the seven Spirits and the seven lamps in our spirit. If we open ourselves daily, then the essence of the stone will get into us. We will be transformed and will enter into the building. This is the coming New Jerusalem. The Spirit of God is the seven lamps, and the church is the seven lampstands. Therefore, the church is the development of the seven Spirits, and the church is entirely a matter in the spirit.

CHAPTER FIVE

IN THE SPIRIT

Scripture Reading: Eph. 3:5; 1:17, 19; 2:22; 3:16-19; 4:22-24; 5:18-19; 6:18-19

THE CHURCH AS THE REPRINT OF THE SPIRIT

We have seen that the reality and substance of the church is the Spirit. In order to clarify this, we may use the three sections of the tabernacle in the Old Testament as an illustration. The outer court, which is outside of the tabernacle itself, denotes the earth, while the Holy Place typifies God's dwelling place in the heavens. The lampstand mentioned in Zechariah 4 denotes the Spirit on the earth, while the lampstand mentioned in Exodus 25 is in the Holy Place and signifies Christ in the heavens. Actually, these lampstands are not two lampstands but two aspects or two ends of the one, unique lampstand in the universe. According to the lampstand's position in the heavens, it is in the Holy Place, but according to its position on the earth, it is outside the Holy Place. The lampstand in the heavens is Christ, and the lampstand on the earth is the Spirit. The Spirit and Christ are not two separate persons. Rather, They are one entity with two aspects. As the One who is with God the Father, He is Christ, but as the One who comes into us, He is the Spirit. We should never separate Christ and the Spirit into two separate persons, because Christ is the Spirit (1 Cor. 15:45b; 2 Cor. 3:17).

As the lampstand He operates on the earth and enters into us, His believers, thus producing the churches, which are also lampstands (Rev. 1:20). In a sense, we may say that there are now seven golden lampstands in the "outer court." The seven golden lampstands in Revelation 1 are the product, expression, and embodiment of the unique golden lampstand. Thus, the church is Christ and the product, embodiment, expression, and manifestation of the Spirit. We must be clear that the substance and reality of the church is the Spirit.

All the lampstands in the Bible are actually one lampstand with three aspects. In one aspect the lampstand is Christ, in another aspect it is the Spirit, and in still another aspect it is the church. Although its aspects are different, its reality or substance is one. The reality and substance of the lampstand is Christ and the Spirit. When we say that the reality of the lampstand is Christ, the emphasis is on the fact, and when we say that the reality of the lampstand is the Spirit, the emphasis is on our experience. According to the fact, the church is Christ, but according to our experience, the church is the embodiment of the Spirit.

We must see that we cannot set up or produce the church by our own effort. Regardless of how much we bear the cross, we cannot produce the church. Regardless of how much we allow ourselves to be crucified on the cross, we cannot produce the church. Regardless of how much we are dealt with, broken, and carved, we are still ourselves and not the church. We do not say this to disparage other Christians. Rather, in saying this we also include ourselves, for we are all God's children. Throughout the centuries God has given His saints vision after vision. Some saw the need to bear the cross, to be broken, and to be dealt with. These matters, however, miss the central point. Strictly speaking, the church is neither a matter of being dealt with nor a matter of bearing the cross and being broken. Rather, it is a matter of the Spirit having a place in us. This is because the essence and reality of the church is the Spirit. For example, the essence or substance of this stand is wood. If the substance of this stand was not wood, then no matter what color you painted it or however you disguised it, it would not be wood. The essence of this stand is wood, and the essence of the church is the Spirit, that is, the Spirit of God. The Spirit of God is God Himself reaching us. However, it was not so simple for God to reach us. He had to go through the process of incarnation, thirty-three and a half years of human living, death, and resurrection to become the life-giving Spirit.

The golden lampstand in Zechariah 4 signifies the Spirit of Jehovah. This golden lampstand signifies Jehovah God who became the life-giving Spirit through incarnation, human living, death, and resurrection. This life-giving Spirit is God Himself. It includes the Father, the Son, and the Spirit and also includes humanity, human living, Christ's mysterious death on the cross, resurrection, and ascension. This is the Triune God who passed through a process to become the all-inclusive Spirit. We may use the making of bread as an illustration. After the wheat in a field ripens and is harvested, it has to be ground into powder, mixed with water, and baked in fire in order to become bread. During the mixing, milk, raisins, and other ingredients may also be added. Consequently, this loaf of bread becomes an all-inclusive loaf of bread. When you eat this bread, you receive all the different kinds of ingredients.

The all-inclusive Spirit includes the Spirit of God in Zechariah 4. This is signified by the lampstand in Zechariah 4, which is for God's building, the church. Hence, the Spirit, signified by the lampstand, is for the producing of the church, which is the reprint of the Spirit. Originally there was only one Spirit, one lampstand, but eventually, seven lampstands were produced. The seven golden lampstands in Revelation 1 and the one golden lampstand in Zechariah 4 are exactly the same. The golden lampstand in Zechariah is the original copy, and the golden lampstands in Revelation are the reprints. The original copy was reprinted, producing seven copies that are exactly like the original. Therefore, the church is the reprint of the Spirit.

May this light shine thoroughly and brightly so that we who are in this age would see more clearly than the Christians twenty years ago. Twenty years ago I spoke concerning the church, but my speaking was not so thorough because I myself did not see the church so clearly. It was only recently that I saw how indispensable the Spirit is. To say that the church is Christ is only to state a fact. If you do not have the dispensing of the Spirit, and if you do not allow the seven

Spirits to shine in you thoroughly, transfusing God into you richly that you may become His reproduction, then you are not in the reality of the church. All you have is a Christian organization or society. There is no reprint of the Spirit and no golden lampstand. The church as the reprint of the Spirit is a lampstand of pure gold.

When this light clearly shines on us, then many of my previous messages and words may become unnecessary. Today we should board the 747 airplane instead of riding on the old oxcart. We must see that the church is the reprint, the expression, and the product of the Spirit. The Spirit is the seven Spirits as the consummation of Jehovah God—the Father, the Son, and the Spirit—who passed through incarnation, human living, death, and resurrection. This Spirit is for the producing of the church.

RECEIVING THE REPRINTING OF THE SPIRIT IN OUR SPIRIT

To print a book or a newspaper, one needs not only a printing plate but also good paper. Suppose you have made a printing plate. If you then try to print something on a piece of glass or on a piece of marble, it will be very difficult. Only when you use a proper sheet of paper will the ink be immediately absorbed and the print will come out clearly. What kind of "paper" is used for the reprint of the Spirit? The "paper" is our spirit! Our mind is like a piece of marble. If you try to understand the spiritual things and the things pertaining to the church with your mind, it is like trying to print a newspaper on marble. It is very difficult, and there is no absorption. Neither can you use your emotion, cleverness, zeal, or good intention to understand spiritual matters. None of these ways will do. For more than forty years I have been observing a group of zealous people. The more zealous they are, the more God has no way in them. Their heart for the church is so good that it is beyond reproach, yet their understanding of the church is so darkened that they hardly know the church. In short, to allow the Spirit to reprint Himself in us, we must be in spirit.

RECEIVING REVELATION IN SPIRIT

There are several passages in Ephesians that mention the phrase *in spirit*. Ephesians 3:5 says that the church as the mystery of Christ has now been revealed in spirit. Within you and me is a mystery that is not known to others. What is this mystery? This mystery is that the Spirit is doing a work of reprinting in our spirit. The Spirit is reprinting the rich Christ and the mysterious God. Such a reprint cannot be touched by the human mind, human wisdom, or human emotion. Only when we are in our spirit can the church as a mystery be revealed to us. This mystery is something altogether in spirit. Thus, we must be in spirit to receive this revelation.

Ephesians 1:17 says that we need a spirit of wisdom and revelation. A spirit of revelation is for seeing, whereas a spirit of wisdom is for understanding. For example, suppose there is a machine that had been covered and kept secret but has now been unveiled and exhibited. This is revelation. However, one may examine it for a long time and still be puzzled as to its use or purpose. One may have the revelation but not the wisdom, and one may have the seeing but not the understanding. Hence, we all need to pray, "O Lord, give us a spirit that can both see and understand." To be in spirit is to be in a spirit of wisdom and revelation. You and I have a spirit within, but this spirit needs to be strengthened and enlightened by the Spirit of God that it may be able to see and understand.

BEING BUILT IN SPIRIT

The church as God's building, God's house, and God's dwelling place is in our spirit. Ephesians 2:22 says, "In whom you also are being built together into a dwelling place of God in spirit." We may say that God dwells in us, but strictly speaking, He does not dwell in our mind or in our emotions but in our spirit. We may say that we are being built together in the church. However, the building is not in our mind but in our spirit. Our mind is wild, like an unbridled horse. Perhaps someone would say to me, "Brother Lee, I am absolutely one with you." Regardless of who he might be, I would not believe him or listen to him, because it is useless for someone to merely say that he is one with me. Being in the mind is not useful, but being in the spirit is useful. If you were truly in spirit, you would be one with me without having to say it. Therefore, our being built together as God's dwelling place can take place only in our spirit. We all have some amount of experience of this. Many times we have opinions, but once we are in spirit, the opinions are gone, and there is no problem. Once we are in spirit, there is the building and the oneness.

BEING STRENGTHENED IN SPIRIT

In Ephesians 3:16 the apostle prayed, "That He would grant you, according to the riches of His glory, to be strengthened with power through His Spirit into the inner man." We need to be strengthened, not in our mind or in our joy, anger, sorrow, or delight but in our spirit, in our inner man. Do not be strong in your mind, will, and emotion. Rather, be strong in spirit. We all need to be strengthened in spirit.

BEING RENEWED IN SPIRIT

Ephesians 4:23 says, "And that you be renewed in the spirit of your mind." What is the spirit of the mind? The mind is the mind, and the spirit is the spirit, but what is the spirit of the mind? This phrase indicates that our spirit has become the spirit of our mind. This means that our spirit is able to control our mind, occupy our mind, and take over our mind. It is good to turn to our spirit, but we need to progress until our spirit controls our mind, that is, until our mind and our spirit are one. It is good to turn to our spirit, but unless our mind is one with our spirit and is under the control of our spirit, our spirit is merely our spirit and not yet the spirit of our mind.

The old man in our conduct is our old manner of life. The new man is the church life. If we allow our spirit to control and direct our mind, our mind and our spirit will become one, and our mind will be subject to our spirit. Spontaneously, we will put off our old manner of life—the old man—and we will put on the new man—the church life. In this way the reality of the church will be expressed through us.

BEING FILLED IN SPIRIT

Ephesians 5:18 says, "Do not be drunk with wine." Wine refers to earthly pleasures. Anything that influences us, drugs us, or affects us is wine. We should not be filled and drunk with earthly pleasures. Verse 18 also says, "But be filled in spirit," that is, be filled unto all the fullness of God (3:19). Wine fills us up physically, causing us to be filled in our body. We should not, however, be filled with wine in our body. Rather, we should be filled unto all the fullness of God in our spirit. This means that we must let go of all the desires of our soul, including our mind, emotion, and will. We should only be filled in spirit unto the fullness of God. The result of this is shown in 5:19, which says, "Speaking to one another in psalms and hymns and spiritual songs, singing and psalming with your heart to the Lord." This is what it means to be filled in our whole being with God. This is what it means when we sing, "And everywhere be Thee and God" (*Hymns,* #489, stanza 8).

PRAYING IN SPIRIT

Ephesians 6:18 says, "Praying at every time in spirit." We should not pray in the mind or in the emotion. Sometimes when others falsely accuse us, we go before God, praying with tears coming down our cheeks. This is not to pray in spirit. If we pray in spirit, we will not shed tears in this way. When we are not in spirit, we feel mistreated and hurt. However, when we turn to our spirit, the Lord does not need to wipe away our tears because our spirit will turn back our tears. We may complain to others about being mistreated, but we cannot go and complain in this way to God. Once we get into the presence of the Lord, that is, once we turn to our spirit, the grievances, insults, suffering, and pain are gone. Nothing matters anymore. Have you had this kind of experience? In the church the sisters often complain that the brothers treat them unfairly. At home the wife often complains that her husband treats her unfairly. However, the moment we turn to our spirit, we can no longer complain or argue. Once we turn to our spirit, we are able to accept others' mistreatment.

Then we are truly bearing the cross. When Paul wrote Ephesians, he did not become long-winded, writing sixty chapters. He wrote only six chapters, which was sufficient. The key is praying "in spirit." Paul knew that if we would pray in spirit, that that would be sufficient.

By reading through the six chapters of Ephesians, we may realize that the reality of the church is entirely in spirit and that the church life should be entirely in spirit. Ephesians, which is a book on the church, mentions one item again and again in every chapter—in spirit. Only in spirit can the church be brought forth. The church cannot be produced through our learning to be broken unless we are in spirit. Perhaps some may say, "If our flesh is broken, then our spirit will be released." However, the problem is that we always focus on the breaking of the outer man instead of focusing on the release of the spirit.

Ephesians does not focus on the negative side of being broken. Instead, it focuses only on the positive side of being in spirit. Our spirit needs to receive the revelation and the wisdom of the Spirit. Our inner man needs to be strengthened. We need to be strengthened and have a spirit of wisdom and revelation. It is in such a spirit that the church life is brought forth. In the previous message we paid attention to the seven Spirits. In this message we are focusing on our spirit. The seven Spirits are the essence and reality of the church, and our spirit is the best "paper" for the reprinting of the seven Spirits. To be the best reprint of the Spirit, we must have a strengthened spirit of wisdom and revelation. In such a spirit, the Spirit will be able to produce the church as His reprint.

CHAPTER SIX

THE ECONOMY OF THE TRIUNE GOD

Scripture Reading: Eph. 3:4-6, 8-11, 16-21

In the preceding messages we have seen God's eternal plan, Christ, the Spirit, and our spirit. These visions have been our focus. In order to meet the need of the Lord's recovery in this age, we as Christians must see these four matters—God's eternal plan, Christ, the Spirit, and our spirit. In this message we will see how God is working Himself into us to make us one with Him so that He may be our life and we may be His expression. We want to see how God carries out this matter.

GOD ACCOMPLISHING HIS ECONOMY IN US
BY THE RICHES OF CHRIST

Ephesians is a great book in the Bible and is filled with great expressions. The first great term used in Ephesians is *mystery*. God has a mystery hidden in Himself (1:9). Another great term is *economy*. God wants us to know what the economy of His hidden mystery is (v. 10). The Greek word that is translated *economy* denotes a kind of management, administration, government, or distribution. God has an economy, and in His economy there is an administration, a government, a dispensation, and a distribution. What is God dispensing and distributing? He is dispensing and distributing Himself into us.

How does God carry out His economy? He carries out His economy by the unsearchable riches of Christ. God has put all that He is, all that He has, and all that He can do into Christ. These are the riches of Christ. All that God is is high, divine, and mysterious, all that God has is bountiful, and all that God can do is boundless. All of this is in Christ as His riches.

We need to see, through a few examples, what God is, what He has, and what He can do. What is God? He is light, love, Spirit, and life. What does God have? He has wisdom, glory, righteousness, and holiness. What can God do? He can call things not being as being, and He can give life to the dead. These are some of the riches of Christ. Paul said that he was sent to preach these riches, that is, to preach what God is, what God has, and what God can do in Christ. God has put all these items in Christ. Thus, this Christ is the embodiment of all that God is, all that God has, and all that God can do. Through His death and resurrection, He became the life-giving Spirit (1 Cor. 15:45b), in whom are all the riches of Christ.

The riches of Christ not only comprise what God is, what God has, and what God can do but also comprise His experiences as a man. Christ is not only God; He is also a man. One day Christ became a man. He went through human living, passed through death, and entered into resurrection. These experiences are also some of the riches of Christ and are now included in the life-giving Spirit. When this Spirit enters into our spirit, we become regenerated in our spirit, and He dwells in our spirit. Now He needs us only to pray.

THE SPIRIT'S STRENGTHENING, CHRIST'S MAKING HIS HOME, AND GOD'S FILLING

We all need to pray the apostle Paul's prayer in Ephesians 3, because his prayer was for God's economy. First, his prayer mentions the Father: "I bow my knees unto the Father...that He..." (vv. 14, 16a). Then, it mentions the Spirit: "To be strengthened with power through His Spirit into the inner man" (v. 16b). Finally, it mentions Christ: "That Christ may make His home in your hearts" (v. 17a). The result is that "you may be filled unto all the fullness of God" (v. 19b). This prayer is truly concerning the Triune God—first concerning the Spirit, then concerning Christ, and lastly concerning God: "To be strengthened with power through His Spirit into the inner man, that Christ may make His home in your hearts...that you may be filled unto all the fullness of God." The Trinity is not merely a doctrine. The Trinity is for God's economy, God's dispensing. God wants to dispense Himself into every one of us. In order to do this, He put all that He is, all that He has, and all that He can do into Christ. Then, Christ became a man, bringing all these items with Him. When He became a man, the element of humanity was added into Him. Afterward, Christ went into death and resurrection, taking with Him both God and man, and through death and resurrection He became the life-giving Spirit. Now it is through this life-giving Spirit that God is working in us.

It is marvelous that the Father strengthens us into our inner man through His Spirit. Our inner man is our spirit. Once we are strengthened into our inner man, Christ comes to make His home in our heart. Thus, we are filled unto the fullness of God. The Spirit's strengthening us is Christ's making His home in us, and Christ's making His home in us is God's filling us. We do not have to wait until we have been strengthened by the Spirit in order for Christ to make His home in us and for God to fill us. The Spirit's strengthening us is Christ's making His home in us, and Christ's making His home in us is God's filling us unto His fullness. These three things are one.

We must see that it is necessary for God to be in Christ, for Christ to be the Spirit, and for the Spirit to enter into our spirit, to operate in us and to strengthen us into our spirit. How does the Spirit strengthen us? He strengthens us by continually supplying us with the riches of Christ. The Spirit's supplying us within is His strengthening us. The more He supplies us, the more we are strengthened, and the more we have Christ's element added to us. Consequently, Christ occupies every part of our being. This is Christ's making His home in us. When Christ occupies our whole being and makes His home in us, we are filled unto all the fullness of God. At this time God is mingled with us. God desires not only to be united with us but also mingled with us.

The Spirit's strengthening us, Christ's making home in us, and God's filling us are not three different matters. This is the Triune God saturating our whole being. The Spirit strengthens us, Christ makes home in us, and God fills us. First He strengthens our spirit, then He enters into our heart, and then He occupies our whole being. This is the Triune God mingling Himself with us.

THE ISSUE OF GOD'S ECONOMY—THE CHURCH

This is not a doctrine; this is God's economy. What is the issue of God's economy? The issue is the church. Therefore, verse 21 says, "To Him be the glory in the church and in Christ Jesus." This is the church life. What is the church? The church is the issue of the Spirit's strengthening us, Christ's making His home in us, and God's filling us. The church is not the result of the breaking of our flesh or the result of the rubbing away of our sharp edges. Some preachers may tell you that because you are a person with many sharp edges, God cannot use you, so He has to raise up situations and use little helpers to knock off your sharp corners and to make you smooth. This kind of teaching is natural and is not taught in the Bible. What the Bible presents is transformation, telling us that we are being transformed from clay to precious stones. May God give us a vision today that we may see what the church is. The church is the result of our being filled, saturated, and occupied by the Triune God as the all-inclusive Spirit.

NOT PAYING ATTENTION TO NEGATIVE DEALINGS

Perhaps some would ask me, "Then what shall we do with our flesh?" The simplest thing to do with the flesh is to put it off. We need to put off the old man and the flesh. We need to put off our peculiarities, our complicated mind, and our stubborn will. Some may say, "I cannot do this." To them I would ask, have you ever seen a tree shedding its bark? The tree continually absorbs water and the riches from the soil, and in this way it is strengthened until it is full-grown. Then it sheds its bark. If we faithfully let the Spirit strengthen us into our inner man, let Christ make His home in our hearts, and let God fill us, then day by day our old man will be gradually put off.

Therefore, instead of paying attention to the negative dealings, we must focus on the positive matters such as the Spirit's strengthening us, Christ's making home in us, and

God's filling us. All of us are peculiar in our natural being. However, God will say to Satan, "Satan, do you see all these peculiar people? I will transform every one of them." God supplies continually, and the result is that the church is produced. Thus, we do not need to deal directly with our peculiarities. Formerly I exerted much effort to deal with my peculiar disposition. Recently, however, my eyes were opened by the Lord to stop trying to deal with my disposition. Therefore, I do not deal with it anymore. We may be able to break a clay pot into pieces and even grind it into powder, but we cannot turn the clay into a diamond. Clay is clay. Therefore, we should give up our dealings. Instead, we should pray for the Spirit's strengthening, Christ's making home, and God's filling, and then the church will be produced.

CHAPTER SEVEN

THE POWER OF RESURRECTION

THE HISTORY OF THE RECOVERY OF SPIRITUAL LIFE

In this message we will fellowship concerning the history of the Lord's recovery of spiritual life. World history calls the centuries leading up to the fifteenth and sixteenth centuries the Dark Ages. Most historians acknowledge the fact that those years were dark, but most do not realize what caused the darkness. We know, however, that the reason those years were dark was because at that time the word of God was completely sealed. Not only was the word of God sealed in letter, it was even physically locked up. The Roman Catholic Church prohibited people from reading the Bible. In their view, only the pope, bishops, and priests were qualified to read the Scriptures, and the interpretation of the Bible was altogether limited to what the pope taught. Hence, the Lord's word, which is the light, was not among the human race at that time. Human history prior to the fifteenth and sixteenth centuries was at its darkest hour.

It was in the sixteenth century that God raised up Martin Luther to bring in the Reformation. The first item God recovered through Luther was the truth of justification by faith. Luther taught that man is saved through justification by faith. This was truly the Lord's doing. However, Protestantism has greatly exaggerated and excessively promoted the recovery of this truth through Luther. Although it was a great move of God, its spiritual value is actually not that great. Although I have not read many of Luther's writings, I have read some of them. Forty to fifty years ago I truly appreciated Luther's writings, but today when I read his books, I feel that they do not mean that much to me. I do not say this because I am proud but because when I read his books, regardless of the subject matter, I touch only doctrines and not life.

Even though his faith and his boldness have been admired by many, he was not always so bold. When the Roman Catholic Church sought to kill him, he relied on Germany's political power for protection. Hence, he betrayed the matter of the church. It is not too much to say this. He betrayed the truth concerning the church in order to gain protection from Germany's political powers.

In any case, when you read Luther's books, you cannot readily find help for your spiritual life. Hence, the result of the Reformation was the coming forth of Sardis. The Lord's word in His epistle to Sardis is, "You have a name that you are living, and yet you are dead" (Rev. 3:1b). Nothing in the midst of Sardis is lively and strong. This is the condition of the Protestant churches. The degradation of the Protestant churches into their present situation did not begin recently. Rather, they became dead and cold shortly after the Reformation began through Luther. The Reformers left the Roman Catholic Church, accepted the doctrine of justification by faith, and even established the so-called Lutheran church. Several northern European countries, such as Germany, Denmark, Sweden, and Norway, accepted the Lutheran church as their state religion. Up to this day the pastors of the German Lutheran church are paid from the treasury of the German government. The kings of Sweden, Denmark, and Norway all serve as the heads of their state churches. The reformers established the Lutheran sect and the Lutheran church, but they sacrificed the truth concerning the church. Hence, from the beginning, even before Luther passed away, the Protestant churches were lifeless.

Church history shows us that God reacted to this situation. There was a reaction of life against the deadness and coldness of the Lutheran doctrines. At that time, both inside and outside of the Catholic Church, there were some reactions of life. While Luther was still alive, several people who were quite strong in life rose up to react to Luther, letting him know that what he taught was all doctrines without life. Luther, however, greatly condemned and opposed them.

One of Luther's contemporaries was a person by the name of Schwenckfeld (1489-1561), who was very strong in life. When I read his books on the experience of life, I noticed that he even referred to the tree of life and to Christ as the life-giving Spirit. Furthermore, he spoke extensively on the condition of Christianity being according to the tree of knowledge of good and evil and on how we can live according to the tree of life by walking according to the Spirit of life and by experiencing Christ. This was a great surprise to me. When we began to see these matters in the Word, we thought we were seeing what no one had ever seen before. Little did we know that Schwenckfeld had seen these things over three hundred years ago. When Schwenckfeld found that Luther would not accept what he had seen, he went into voluntary exile, which lasted for many years. Luther rejected his attempt at reconciliation, calling him a fool possessed by the devil. From this we can begin to understand why fundamental Christianity opposes us when we get into matters such as the Spirit of life. While the emphasis of fundamental Christianity is on doctrines, the emphasis of the Lord's reaction is on life.

At that time God raised up people in the Roman Catholic Church such as Madame Guyon who also reacted in life. These people are called the mystics in church history. They reacted in life but were not very clear about the truth. Hence, their teachings and applications became mysterious. Furthermore, the experiences of Madame Guyon and Thomas à Kempis, author of *The Imitation of Christ,* leaned heavily toward asceticism. The teachings of the mystics, however, greatly influenced Protestantism. Those in the Protestant churches did not appreciate Schwenckfeld because he had been condemned by Luther, whom they highly respected. Therefore, they turned their attention to the mystical teachings of those such as Madame Guyon. Most people, however, did not know how to apply mysticism, which, though it contained some genuine things, was too mysterious.

In the last century William Law was raised up in Great Britain. He was a highly intelligent and very knowledgeable person and was also a proficient writer and capable speaker. In the first stage of his life, he laid great emphasis on doctrines, but one day his eyes were opened to see the inner life. At that moment he was completely changed and had a complete turn. After he experienced such a turn, he began to appreciate the teachings of mysticism, and he also simplified them, making them practical. Hence, it was through him that the teachings of mysticism spread out. Andrew Murray, who was also raised up by the Lord, received great help from him. The main matter that Andrew Murray learned was fellowship with the Lord, that is, contact with the Lord through prayer in spirit. He paid much attention to the matters of the power of the Holy Spirit, the filling of the Holy Spirit, and the fellowship of the Holy Spirit. Among those who received help from him, the most prominent one was Mrs. Penn-Lewis. She was also the one who saw the most in her time concerning the cross. She saw a great deal and also spoke a great deal. Unfortunately, because she saw the cross and knew spiritual warfare, she became too affected by these matters and turned her attention to the matter of demons, thereby neglecting the development of life. Consequently, her feelings and thoughts were mostly concerning demons. Her case became something truly pitiful.

Around 1925 the Lord used some whom He had raised up on the earth to show the church the resurrection of Christ. When these ones saw it and spoke it, they were in spirit. With time, however, the principles of resurrection became empty doctrines. Hence, those who listened to them received merely doctrines.

Then the Lord brought a sister by the name of M. E. Barber to China. I do not believe she received anything from Schwenckfeld, so except for the things of Schwenckfeld, she brought all the items that we have mentioned to China and genuinely practiced them. She also shared all these things with Brother Watchman Nee, who was greatly helped by her. This was the way the Lord took.

Through Brother Nee, the Lord gradually went on step by step. Based on what I observed while I stayed by Brother Nee's side, I concluded that what he genuinely saw and knew in his last years is partially represented by the book *The Breaking of the Outer Man and the Release of the Spirit.* Today when many people read this book, they overemphasize the breaking of the outer man and neglect the release of the spirit. Before that book was published in 1948, I had much contact with him in Shanghai for two years, and in our conversations he kept saying that our spirit must be released whether we are praying, preaching, or talking to people. He said, however, that it is often difficult for our spirit to be released. Hence, God raises up certain situations to break our outer man. Thus, the breaking of the outer man is not the goal. If we would release our spirit, there would be no need for the breaking. When some people read *The Breaking of the Outer Man and the Release of the Spirit,* they hold on to certain pages, chapters, or sections where Brother Nee speaks about being broken. However, he spoke about being broken for the release of the spirit, not for the sake of being broken. Nonetheless, when many people read this book, they pay attention to the breaking of the outer man and neglect the release of the spirit.

Brother Nee repeatedly stated that the human spirit must be released. Only when our spirit is released, can the Holy Spirit come forth, because the Holy Spirit is imprisoned in our spirit. He also realized that the Holy Spirit is the reality of everything. He realized that no matter how much you speak concerning the cross, you cannot have the reality of the cross if you do not have the Holy Spirit. Regardless of how much you talk about life, you cannot have life apart from the Holy Spirit of God. You may speak a great deal about Christ, but if you do not have the Holy Spirit, you do not have the reality of Christ. Brother Nee realized that the Holy Spirit is the reality of all spiritual matters, and he also recognized the need for the release of the spirit. Thus, we can see the importance of the two spirits—the Holy Spirit and our human spirit.

A PERSONAL TESTIMONY
OF TURNING TO THE SPIRIT

What I would like to share with you now is a personal

testimony of turning to the spirit. I hope that you will take it in and be impressed with it. I began to preach in Taiwan in 1949, and in 1958 I reached a turning point. At that time there was a storm in our midst. After observing the situation from many angles, I realized that although many had heard the doctrine of the cross and had even preached it, they still did all sorts of negative things. I was greatly troubled by this and asked myself whether or not the cross was truly effective. Furthermore, I also observed those who had learned about the principle of resurrection life. They preached the doctrine concerning this matter, but in the way they conducted themselves, in their daily walk they were void of resurrection and life. Hence, within me I had a big question mark concerning the doctrines of the cross and resurrection.

Because I was greatly disturbed by these matters, I did not trust in these doctrines anymore. Therefore, from February through April of 1958, in at least three or four consecutive conferences, the Lord began to release messages among us saying that doctrines are futile and that we must eat the Lord, drink the Lord, and enjoy the Lord. If you read the books put out by us, you will see that before 1958 we did not have such expressions and utterances as *eating the Lord, drinking the Lord,* and *enjoying the Lord.* These messages were later published in a book titled *How to Enjoy God.* [This book has not yet been published in English.—trans.] Ever since the Lord brought about this turn in me, I have no longer preached doctrines of knowledge. No matter how much you preach the dealing of the cross, and no matter how much you preach concerning resurrection life, it is of no profit. The only thing that is profitable is the Lord Himself in us becoming not only our life but also our life supply. When we live by Him, what we live out is the genuine life, the genuine spirituality, and the genuine church life. If we are not in spirit, what we do may be more evil than what unbelievers do. Regardless of how many years you have been saved, if you do not live in spirit, you are capable of doing any kind of evil thing.

Hence, in 1958 I had a turn within. I turned from expounding doctrines to paying attention to the spirit. The Lord has shown me that in our relationship with Him, in our spiritual life, and in our church life, everything hinges on Him as the Spirit entering into our spirit and upon our living by this Spirit to enjoy all His riches. From that time onward I have been constantly turning. Even until now I feel that the turning has not stopped but is still going on.

OUR NATURAL CONCEPT
STRESSING NEGATIVE DEALINGS

Why do we so easily lean toward matters such as the dealing, breaking, and suffering of the cross? This is because these things correspond to, and are very close to, our natural concept. We must be cautious when learning the lessons of being broken and being dealt with. If we overemphasize them, we may easily fall into Hinduism, which mainly teaches people to suffer hardship and to be saved through suffering. There is a certain famous preacher in India who brought all these Hindu teachings on suffering into Christianity. As a result, today many Hindus have accepted Christianity, but their practical lives are still according to the Hindu practice of suffering. The Chinese people are similar. Chinese culture is a combination of Confucianism and Buddhism. Confucianism stresses the improvement of behavior, whereas Buddhism emphasizes suffering. These two "isms" form the Chinese ideology and philosophy. This kind of ideology and philosophy was passed down from our ancestors and has become deeply rooted in us so that we still have these things within us, more or less. Even many Westerners are like this. Church history tells us that in the beginning the Roman Catholic Church taught people to improve their conduct by enduring sufferings. They even had a special kind of chair with many spikes that people would sit on when they were aroused in their fleshly lusts.

Matters such as suffering, behavior improvement, being broken, being dealt with, and bearing the cross correspond to our natural concept but are lacking in revelation. The book of Ephesians, on the other hand, is not according to our natural concept but is full of revelation. In Ephesians the cross is mentioned only once in relation to the fact that Christ has slain the enmity through the cross (2:16). The cause of this enmity was the law of the commandments in ordinances. The enmity was slain not for redemption or for salvation but for the Jews and the Gentiles to be created in Himself into one new man. In Ephesians 4 there is a word concerning putting off the old man as regards the former manner of life and being renewed in the spirit of the mind (vv. 22-23). Chapter five speaks about cleansing the church by the washing of the water in the word and removing the spots and wrinkles (vv. 26-27). If you read Ephesians again, you will notice that this book, which speaks specifically concerning the church and the church life, speaks very little about negative things.

EPHESIANS BEING
FULL OF POSITIVE REVELATIONS

Let us consider the positive matters that are revealed in Ephesians. Chapter one says that the church is the Body of Christ, the fullness of the One who fills all in all (v. 23). The Brethren saw the matter of the church as the Body of Christ as early as the nineteenth century. However, they never said that the Body grows by feeding on the riches of Christ. Every mother knows that children need the supply of food to grow. If there is no supply, how can the Body grow? Therefore, chapter three speaks concerning the riches of Christ (v. 8). If you read all the books in Christianity, you would not find one book on the unsearchable riches of Christ. Even our books prior to 1960 never mentioned the unsearchable riches of Christ. This was because in those days we did not sufficiently see the positive side. We mentioned the Body of Christ, but after a certain amount of speaking, we reverted back to speaking about the cross. We said that without the dealing of the cross we could not become the Body of Christ. We also said that if we are not broken, it will be difficult for us to be in coordination with others. If we were all broken by the cross, could the Body of Christ be produced simply by our coming together? It could not. The Body of Christ in chapter one grows by feeding on the riches of Christ in chapter three. Suppose you have a newborn child who is less than twenty-four inches long and weighs only six and a half pounds. If you spanked him every day to make him bear the cross and to cause him to be dealt with, I am afraid that in less than three weeks you would have to hold a funeral for him. It would be better to permit him to be a little bit naughty and to make him eat plenty of food so that he may become strong. If he is disobedient, you may have to discipline him, but afterward you should make him eat some more. The point is to get him to eat. If you only discipline him, "break" him, and deal with him, but do not give him anything to eat, he will be finished. He will be dealt with so severely that he will be skinny, pale, and dry.

Ephesians chapter one is on the Body of Christ, whereas chapter three is on the riches of Christ. What does chapter four speak about? Chapter four speaks about the Body arriving at a full-grown man, at the measure of the stature of the fullness of Christ. How does the Body grow? The Body grows by receiving the supply. Ephesians does not mention dealings. It speaks only of the supply. Paul preached to us the unsearchable riches of Christ that we "may be filled unto all the fullness of God" (3:19b). This is the supply.

In the past when we spoke on Ephesians, we spoke concerning the Body, but we did not preach the riches of Christ. We spoke concerning the growth, yet we did not touch the matter of how we may be filled unto the fullness of God. In other words, we did not see that the church is produced by being supplied with the riches of Christ. Many of our hymns, such as those on the exhibition of Christ and the enjoyment of the riches of the land of Canaan, were written after 1960. Prior to 1960, these matters were not in our literature. When we mentioned anything in our books about Canaan before 1960, we said that it referred to the air, which is the spiritual battleground, because there were seven tribes in Canaan, typifying the spiritual forces of evil in the air. Therefore, we spoke concerning fighting the battle there daily. In the past we never told people how rich the produce of the land of Canaan was or how we should bring the produce to God and enjoy it with God, thereby bringing forth spiritual worship and a corporate life before God. We did not say these kinds of things prior to 1960.

The Lord is truly advancing. In the last fifteen years He has advanced quite far. We must endeavor to catch up with the present age. We do not mean that what we taught in the past was wrong, but the past is the past. The past cannot match today. Today we see the positive side of spiritual matters. Today in the book of Ephesians, I focus solely on the positive things instead of on the negative things.

The Body of Christ is produced not by our teachings or by our cultivation and much less by our being dealt with. The Body of Christ comes out of the supply of the riches of Christ. In chapter one we see the Body, in chapter three we see the riches, and in chapter four we see the growth. It is not a matter of being dealt with, of being broken, or of bearing the cross. In the previous message we saw that it is by the Spirit's strengthening us into our inner man, Christ's making His home in our hearts, and God's filling us that the church is produced.

Furthermore, in the past we saw the church only as the Body, but we did not have much impression of the church as the new man. The Body needs the supply of the riches, but the new man needs someone to be his person. No matter how much we are dealt with, we cannot produce a person. We may bear the cross daily, but we cannot produce a person. The person of the new man does not come from our being dealt with, being broken, or bearing the cross. Rather, this person is the all-inclusive Christ becoming our indwelling person. I hope that from now on we would completely turn to the positive things. Whenever we sit down together to fellowship, we should share about how Christ is making His home in us to be our person, declaring, "Hallelujah, the Lord of all lives in me!"

Formerly we overstressed the first part of Galatians 2:20, which says, "I am crucified with Christ; and it is no longer I who live...." It is true that it is "no longer I," but who is it then? We did not pay enough attention to the next phrase, which says, "But it is Christ." It is not merely His power or His virtues but Christ Himself! It is Christ who lives in us, yet we neglected this matter. Whether or not we are crucified, Christ is in us, and Christ lives in us. He is not only our life but also our person making His home in us. Today the Lord is taking us onward in a definite way. We must look at the positive side. We must put together the crucial items in each chapter of Ephesians. Is the Christ who is making His home in us a poor man? No! The Christ who is making His home in us is unsearchably rich. If our wife bothers us, why should we determine to endure the pain and take up our wife as a cross when the unsearchable riches of Christ within us can be our supply? We should enjoy Christ more so that we may supply our wife. We should change our concept and our speaking and say to her, "Oh, dear wife, I have treated you wrongly. From the day we got married, I have been taught to take you as my cross. Since then, I have truly wronged you in bearing you as my cross. Today, however, I declare to you good news of great joy: you are not my cross but rather my joy and my comfort!" When we get married, we do not need our wife to be a cross to deal with us. Rather, we need our wife to be our co-enjoyer because Christ is so rich! I am afraid that some of the sisters are still bearing the cross. Quickly lay the "cross" aside, consecrate this matter, and let us enjoy Christ. Christ, who is unsearchably rich, is making His home in us that we may be filled unto all the fullness of God.

I am full of regret that my messages in the past brought you much hardship. I often said that your wives were your crosses and that some of you, due to your strong dispositions, needed not only a wife but also several children. I also warned you that by marrying, you get yourself into bondage and chains. Now I would like to tell you that the marriage life is a life of happiness. However, it is a life of happiness not in the flesh but in enjoying and sharing Christ together. I would like to annul the teachings I gave in the past. Do not come to me and say, "Brother Lee, did you not teach concerning the cross before?" Yes, I taught in that way before, but today—September 4, 1975—I solemnly declare that those teachings are annulled. I do not annul all the previous teachings, only the teachings concerning bearing the cross and suffering hardship. Empty yourself and come take in something positive. The church is the Body of Christ, which is supplied by Christ daily. When we eat the riches of Christ, we become healthy and strong. In the local churches there should be no "little caterpillars." Rather, we should all be tall and strong as a result, not of being taught, but of eating Christ. The Spirit's strengthening us, Christ's making His home in us, and God's filling us issue in the church.

THE POWER OF SURPASSING GREATNESS

Ephesians 1:17-20 says, "That the God of our Lord Jesus Christ, the Father of glory, may give to you a spirit of wisdom and revelation in the full knowledge of Him, the eyes of your heart having been enlightened, that you may know what is the hope of His calling, and what are the riches of the glory of His inheritance in the saints, and what is the surpassing greatness of His power toward us who believe, according to the operation of the might of His strength, which He caused to operate in Christ in raising Him from the dead and seating Him at His right hand in the heavenlies." We all need to learn to eat these words. Here Paul wants us to see the power of surpassing greatness. The word *power* is a very particular word. The literal translation of the Greek word is *dynamo*. A dynamo is a dynamic power, an exploding power. This is the power according to the might of His strength. The word *operate,* which also means "energize," is also a literal translation of the Greek word. According to the might of His strength, God caused the power to be energized in Christ in raising Him from the dead. Christ's being raised from the dead is not a simple matter. He was raised not only from the tomb but also from the dead. The dead are in Hades, which has the power to hold the dead. Acts 2:24 says, however, that it was not possible for Christ to be held by death. He broke forth from the imprisonment of death and Hades. Today this great power is also operating in us.

Furthermore, this mighty power also seated Christ at God's right hand in the heavenlies. This shows us Christ's ascendancy and transcendence. Moreover, He is far above all rule and authority and power and lordship and every name that is named not only in this age but also in that which is to come. We know that gravity is a tremendously great force. Christ in His resurrection and ascension overcame three layers of forces. The first layer—Hades, the power of death—is underneath the earth. The second layer—the force of gravity—is on the earth. The third layer is the obstruction from the rulers and authorities in the air. After His resurrection, the Lord Jesus overcame Hades, the earth's gravity, and the rulers and authorities of the air. Then He ascended to the heavenlies. How surpassing is the greatness of His power!

Furthermore, God subjected all things under Christ's feet and gave Christ to be Head over all things to the church. This is the great power that operated in Christ. Hallelujah, this great power is also in us today!

Ephesians 3:20 says, "But to Him who is able to do superabundantly above all that we ask or think, according to the power which operates in us." God's doing is not according to the power from heaven or according to the power from an outside source but according to the power that operates in us. There is a dynamo in every one of us. Verse 16 says, "That He would grant you, according to the riches of His glory, to be strengthened with power through His Spirit." The Greek word for *power* can also be translated *dynamo*. It is according to this power that God is able to do superabundantly above all that we ask or think. Every one of us has this power within us, like a generator running inside of us. Unfortunately, instead of turning on the generator inside us, we often pay attention to the outward dealings. Consequently, the power that should be operating in us is inoperative. What is it to exercise the spirit and to turn to our spirit? It is to forget about everything outward and to turn on the generator. When we turn on the switch, the generator inside immediately starts to run.

We must see that Christ in us has unsearchable riches. We must also see that the all-inclusive Spirit in us is a dynamo. It is not a matter of how we act outwardly, how we behave outwardly, or how we improve ourselves. It is a matter of turning on the generator inside. Once the generator inside is turned on and starts running, it generates the power of surpassing greatness. This power is so great that there is no way to describe it other than to say, "What surpassing greatness!" This great power enabled Christ to overcome Hades, the force of gravity, and the evil authorities in the air. It enabled Christ to ascend to the highest place in the universe and then to enter into our spirit. What great power this is! Today this dynamo is in us.

Chapter Eight

THE PERFECTING OF THE GIFTS

OUR NATURAL CONCEPT HINDERING US FROM RECEIVING REVELATION

Ephesians is a book that requires revelation because the matters it speaks about are high and profound and are not according to our natural concepts or religious thoughts. For this reason we may read Ephesians once, twice, or even a hundred times without anything echoing within our being. Because we are so full of natural concepts and religious ideas, anything that corresponds with them will immediately cause an echo and find a place in our being, even if we have never heard of it beforehand. Thus, we have not paid much attention to the matters in Ephesians. By the Lord's mercy, we have seen quite a few things from Ephesians in the past and have also released and presented these things to the saints. Nevertheless, after these things were presented, they were neglected. We have not paid much attention to them in our daily living, not to mention in the meetings.

When we are stirred up to love and seek the Lord, our heart toward Him is right. However, after some pursuing, our concepts and ideas spontaneously turn to the cultivation of our conduct, because of the lack of light and revelation. The whole human race has the natural concept of cultivating their conduct. Because religion has been influencing mankind for several thousand years, the concepts of asceticism, behavior improvement, and the cultivation of one's conduct have penetrated all fallen people. Moreover, the Bible contains numerous passages that apparently resemble the teachings concerning cultivating one's conduct and practicing asceticism. Hence, it is very easy for us to fall into these things. For example, when we read Brother Nee's book *The Breaking of the Outer Man and the Release of the Spirit,* most of us immediately turn our attention to the breaking of the outer man and disregard the release of the spirit. Brother Nee said that the spirit cannot be released if the outer man is not broken. Thus, the outer man must be broken. When we hear this, most of us immediately focus on the breaking and forget about whether or not the spirit is released.

During the last half century, beginning with Mrs. Penn-Lewis, the teaching concerning the cross was widely propagated. Consequently, it is common for people to desire to be broken by the cross and to learn the lesson of the cross. However, the result of all the breaking and learning is rather empty. In the United States I have stayed in the homes of many typical American Christians who were zealously loving and seeking the Lord. In every home there were shelves of spiritual books, which would invariably include books by Mrs. Penn-Lewis. Some of the Christians had actually read all her books. Yet there was no cross in their practical living. Again, this confirmed my observation that merely having the teachings concerning the cross and resurrection is futile. We must be in spirit to have the reality. When we are taught matters such as practicing asceticism, being broken, and learning the lesson of the cross, we find that these things correspond to our natural concepts and are easily absorbed. However, when we are taught matters such as touching the spirit or seeing the riches of Christ, most of us are like pieces of marble that cannot easily absorb ink. Our inner concepts cannot assimilate these things. However, these are the very items that the Lord wants to recover. He will keep coming back to touch us about them.

THE NEED TO SEE THE RICHES
AND THE POWER OF CHRIST

My deep feeling is that it would be a shame in the Lord's recovery if the church was poor and weak. Chapter three of Ephesians speaks of the unsearchable riches of Christ. Paul has already preached these riches to us. Thus, these unsearchable riches are already in the church. Ephesians chapter three not only speaks of the unsearchable riches of Christ but also of His great power, that is, the dynamo, the exploding power, the energizing power of Christ. This great power is in us as well. Thus, we should be rich, and we also should be strengthened by this great power. Many times, however, we seem to be poor and weak, and this even becomes our boast and excuse, as well as our slogan by which to plead with others for sympathy and understanding. How pitiful this is! We all need to read Ephesians chapter three concerning the unsearchable riches and the great power again. We must declare, "The church is not poor! The church is not weak! In the church are the unsearchable riches of Christ and also the great power of Christ's resurrection, ascension, and transcendence."

Ephesians chapter one says that the church is the Body of Christ. Chapter two says that the church is the new man. The church is not only the Body of Christ but also the new man. We have pointed out that a person cannot be made to grow by beating him or telling him to learn certain lessons. If he is not well-fed and nourished, he will not be healthy, no matter how much he learns about health and personal hygiene or how much he exercises. If you do not give a child enough to eat and only discipline him, telling him to learn certain lessons and to exercise, you are actually helping him to die faster. For a child to grow and stay healthy, what he needs to do is not to learn certain lessons but to eat. If he is fed, he will be healthy. If a child is not fed, he cannot grow, and if he does not grow, you cannot teach him to do anything. What a person needs first is not teachings but the proper eating. The church is the Body of Christ and also the new man. The church as the Body and the new man needs to grow, and growth requires eating. This is not a doctrine. Teachings will not make a person grow. In order for a person to grow, he must eat, and he must eat adequately. There is no other way. Even an old man who does not need to grow bigger still needs to eat a large amount of food. Just as a car needs to be filled with gas for a long trip, every day I need to eat three full meals. Then I am able to work all day long with vigor.

Ephesians chapter one speaks about the Body, chapter two speaks about the new man, and chapter three speaks about the unsearchable riches of Christ and His great power. This is the "gas station" of the church. The economy of God is to dispense His unsearchable riches and the great power of His resurrection into us. Do you realize that you have the unsearchable riches of Christ and His great power in you? Most of us are foolishly blind to this fact. We have often said that the Lord dwells in us. Since the Lord dwells in us, His riches and His great power must also be in us. We all have these riches and this great power in us.

The riches and the great power in chapter three are for the Body in chapter one and the new man in chapter two. When we enjoy the riches and the power within, the church is produced. What is the church? The church is the Body and the new man. How does the church grow? The church grows by the riches of Christ, which are not only for nourishment but also for power. When a person has enough to eat, he has strength. Hence, the power comes from the riches. We must see all these points.

HUMAN PERFECTING BEING UNABLE TO MANIFEST THE FUNCTIONS OF THE MEMBERS

The church is both the Body and the new man, and it grows by the riches and the power that are in the church. Now we need to see that the members need to function. After we receive the riches and the power, our feet can walk, our hands can do things, our eyes can look at people, and our mouth can speak. When we eat well and grow, our body is able to function. Therefore, Ephesians chapter four speaks about functions, telling us how every member of the Body manifests its function.

Allow me to tell you frankly that the churches in the Orient all pay too much attention to work, laying stress on doing this and doing that and hoping that by doing so the saints will be perfected. This is not the way to perfect the saints as revealed in Ephesians 4. Suppose there is a child who is small and skinny. For this child to grow, he must have ears that can hear, eyes that can see, a nose that can smell, a mouth that can eat and speak, hands that can do things, and feet that can run. However, if this little child cannot do these things, what shall we do? Suppose we divided his members into groups. We put the nose, eyes, and mouth into one group and then we worked on them to perfect them so that the nose would learn to smell, the eyes would learn to see, and the mouth would learn to speak. Do you think this kind of perfecting by grouping will be helpful? If you left the child in this situation, he would probably live a few more days. But after all your doings, eventually he will be dead. Methods like this are merely human works. I have stated that the cultivation of our conduct, the cross, and brokenness can only produce man-made improvement, man-made godliness, man-made spirituality, and man-made victory. Now I would even say that all the groupings are also man-made.

THE WAY FOR THE GENUINE PERFECTING OF THE GIFTS

The Giving of Grace and the Measure of the Gift

How do we perfect our gifts? We should begin by pray-reading Ephesians 4:7-16. This is a difficult section to understand. It begins by saying that God has given grace to each one of us according to the measure of the gift of Christ. What is the gift of Christ? Every one of us who is saved is a gift given by Christ to the church. Paul was a gift given by Christ to the church, and so are you. You may say that you are only a little member, but even the little members are gifts given by Christ to the Body. When my ear itches, I can conveniently scratch it with my little finger. Thus, I have deeply realized that my little finger is truly a precious gift given to me by the Creator. Every member of our body is a gift given to us by the Creator.

Due to some recent problems with my eyes, I have begun to realize how precious my eyes are. It would be a real misery to me to lose my eyes. The Creator has given our body two little eyes as a lovely gift. Every part of our body, without exception, is a gift. Suppose we only had a piece of skin instead of a nose on our face. How miserable we would be!

Thus, the nose is also a gift. Every saved person is a member of the Body of Christ, and every member is a gift given by the Head to the Body. Do not consider yourself unimportant even if you are only a little brother. The church needs little brothers like you. As a little brother you are a gift of Christ.

Each member of the body has its measure. The measure of the little finger is rather small, but the measure of the arm is larger. The eyes have a certain measure, and the ears also have a certain measure. This is the measure of the gift.

Grace was given to us according to the measure of the gift. Based on Ephesians 3, grace is the unsearchable riches of Christ plus His great power enjoyed by us. We are both the Body and the new man, and the riches of Christ and His great power are our supply. When this supply comes into us, that is grace. For example, the food we eat first reaches our stomach, and after it is digested by the stomach, the nutrients are transfused into every member of our body according to the measure of each member.

Each Member Growing and Being Perfected through the Supply

It is this supply that causes each member to become a useful and functioning member. For example, suppose there is a young brother who is small and skinny. Suppose that he can neither hear nor see clearly and that his nose and mouth do not function properly. We should not try to teach him, work on him, or perfect him. If we truly want to perfect him, every day we should feed him, not only three meals but even seven meals a day. If he is fed daily, he will grow daily. Then one day his ears will be able to hear, his eyes will be able to see, his nose will be able to smell, and he will be able to do things with his hands and walk with his feet. Every member of his body will function. If the church does not supply the believers with the riches of Christ, it is impossible for them to be perfected. Outward perfecting amounts to nothing. The genuine perfecting is accomplished by feeding the members.

How do we know that the perfecting in 4:12 is feeding? We know because growth is mentioned later in the chapter. What is the way to make a person's body grow? There is no other way besides eating. Only eating can cause a person's body to grow. When a person grows, every member of his body functions.

Many times we hope that the brothers and sisters will open their mouths and function in the meetings. Some of them, however, have not received any supply for two and a half years. Since they have not been fed and are not growing, they cannot function.

The sequence of the first four chapters of Ephesians is as follows. Chapter one is on the Body, chapter two is on the new man, and chapter three is on the supply, that is, the riches of Christ and His great power. Then in chapter four the functions of all the members become manifest. The functions are not manifested by receiving teachings or by outwardly learning certain lessons. The functions are manifested through the supply of grace within. Suppose a young brother is led to learn the lessons of daily being broken, bearing the cross, being pressed, and weeping. If you wanted him to stand up and speak after two years of this kind of learning, all he would be able to do would be to weep before you. He would have nothing to minister if he stood up. He would have nothing to minister or to say. Suppose, however, that he begins to enjoy the riches of Christ and experience the power of Christ daily. Then there would be no need to wait for two and a half years for him to function. In two and a half days he would come to the meeting jumping and speaking. If we want to function in the meetings, we must grow. I hope we can all see this secret.

Making Captives Gifts

Immediately after saying that grace was given to us according to the measure of the gift, Paul told us where the gifts come from. He said that Christ led a train of vanquished foes. This indicates that when Christ ascended to the heavens, He was like a victorious general returning triumphantly and leading a train of captives. When Christ ascended to the heavens, we did not see Him, but all the angels saw Him leading a train of captives. In this train of captives were the devil, the fallen angels, and human beings, including you and me. We must realize that we were formerly Christ's enemies and were all in the same train with the devil and the rebellious angels. We had joined their company and were associated with them. They opposed Christ, and so did we. Christ, however, vanquished all these foes and made them captives.

Christ brought these captives with Him in His ascension and gave gifts to men. For many years I read this word but could not understand it. One day the Lord showed me that out of His train of captives He chose a group of people, among whom were Saul of Tarsus, you, and me. Then He made these captives gifts. Saul of Tarsus had been an opposer of the Lord. However, the Lord took him captive, worked on him, and made him a gift. Then He gave him to the Body, which is the church.

I believe that many of you were also opposers of Christ, but Christ captured you. Christ further selected you from the train of captives, worked on you, and gave you to the church as a gift. Then He worked on another one and gave him to the church as a gift. I can testify that fifty years ago He worked on me. At that time I was a wild horse who knew only to run hastily to the world. Nevertheless, He worked in me, and I became a captive in His train. Then He worked in me further and gave me to His church as one of His gifts.

Of course, it is not a simple matter for the Lord to give us sinners as gifts to the Body, His church. He does not simply look at you and, if He likes you, pick you up with His right hand and give you to the church with His left hand, thereby making you a gift. It is not so fast or simple. When He looks at you with His eyes, He infuses you with Himself as the Spirit. When He looks at you, the Spirit gets into you, and you become captivated by Him. Do you realize that all of us believers have been captivated by Him? I have been captivated, and I took the lead to be captivated by Him. Consider yourselves, have you not all been captivated by Him? Today many of the college students have some scientific knowledge. Since you have this knowledge, some may wonder why you are so involved with Jesus and why you go to the meeting hall every day. It is because you have been captivated! People who have not been captivated by the Lord are not able to understand what we are doing. They simply cannot understand why we can never stop reading the Bible. We have indeed been captivated by the Lord, because by His one look He has infused Himself into us as the Spirit. We cannot help behaving in this way because something has come into us. What came into us is not just life or just the Spirit. We have also received the riches of Christ and His great power. The Lord uses what we have received to work in us.

The church is the Body of Christ. The Body is sustained by Christ's unsearchable riches and upheld by His resurrection power. Hence, we should be in the third heaven every day. Christ is on the throne, and we should also be on the throne. Even if there is a heavy burden on us, it should be a footstool underneath our feet. There should be no pain. There should be only Christ's riches and power. This is what has been transfused into us and what makes us gifts. Some of us have been made apostles, some prophets, some evangelists, and some shepherds. These ones who have been made gifts in turn work together with the Head on others. This is their perfecting of the saints.

The Key to Perfecting—Feeding

How do these ones perfect the saints? They do not tell the saints to learn certain lessons or to endure meaningless sufferings. Rather, they feed the saints and minister Christ to them. The word *perfecting* in the phrase *for the perfecting of the saints* (Eph. 4:12a) implies feeding. Perfecting can be understood as feeding. How do we know that the perfecting here refers to feeding? It is because the following verse says that we will eventually arrive at a full-grown man, at the measure of the stature of the fullness of Christ, which is the church. The stature of Christ has a measure, and we all must arrive at the measure of the stature of the fullness of Christ. In order to arrive at this stage, we must eat. We need to eat, eat, eat! If we eat, we will grow, and we will arrive at a full-grown man, at the measure of the stature of the fullness of Christ. Eventually, we will no longer be little children tossed by waves and carried about by every wind of teaching in the sleight of men. Rather, we will hold to the reality, which is Christ, in love. Holding to Christ in love, we will grow up into Him in all things.

Verse 16, the last verse of this section, says that out from the Head all the Body is being joined together and knit together through every joint of the rich supply and through the operation in the measure of each one part. At this stage we have the joints of supply among us. Not only are the joints themselves fed, they can also minister to others. Then every part has its measure from which the function is produced. Finally, all the members are gifts, and all manifest their functions. The functioning of all the members causes the growth of the Body.

The members manifest their functions because they have been nourished with Christ. Once they have been nourished, their function is to help others to eat. Hence, this causes the Body to grow and build up itself in love. There is no need to have pastors or preachers. The only need is that all the members be nourished and grow. Then they can minister to others and cause the Body to grow and build itself up in love.

The key to this portion is eating. Eating affords us the supply of grace. What is the supply of grace? It is the riches of Christ and the power of His resurrection. Therefore, chapter one speaks of the Body, chapter two speaks of the new man, chapter three speaks of the supply, and chapter four speaks of the growth and the manifestation of the functions. In this way the church life is brought forth. Hence, the latter half of chapter four says that we should put off the old man and put on the new man to have the church life. This is produced not by being taught, by being dealt with, or by learning certain lessons. None of these things can help us. We need to enjoy the riches of Christ in our inner man and enjoy His power as our supply of grace that each one of us may grow and that our function may be manifested. We also need to minister to others in order to cause the growth of the Body unto the building up of itself in love.

CHAPTER NINE

WASHING, NOURISHING, AND CHERISHING

Scripture Reading: Eph. 5:25-27, 29

NATURAL CONCEPTS HINDERING US
FROM RECEIVING REVELATION

In the previous message we said, by way of indication, by way of inference, that the matter of eating is referred to in Ephesians chapter four. If we want to grow, we must eat, for our body grows by our eating. Ephesians 4 reveals that the perfecting of the gifts is to cause us to grow up into the Head, Christ, in all things. Based upon this we saw that we must eat if we want to grow. We also saw a little concerning the matter of eating.

In John 6 the Lord Jesus said, "He who eats Me, he also shall live because of Me" (v. 57b). This word is figurative. It does not mean that the Lord really wanted people to take one or two bites of Him. What He meant was that He wanted them to receive Him into them. The basic principle of eating is to take something outside of you and assimilate it into your blood cells that it may become a part of you. Actually, the Lord did not stress eating itself. He stressed the underlying principle of eating, which is to take Him into us that He may become us. This was the Lord's intention when He spoke about eating.

Unfortunately, that day the Jews misunderstood the Lord's words. They said, "How can this man give us His flesh to eat?" (v. 52). Even many of His disciples said, "This word is hard; who can hear it?" (v. 60). In response to these words, the Lord said, "It is the Spirit who gives life; the flesh profits nothing" (v. 63a). Moreover, sympathizing with their weakness,

He went on to say, "The words which I have spoken to you are spirit and are life" (v. 63b). Although the Lord spoke these words, Christianity has made the Lord's words into doctrine. In Christianity today the Lord's words are neither spirit nor life but have become letter, doctrine, knowledge, and death. Therefore, we really need a spirit of wisdom and revelation, which the apostle Paul prays at the beginning of Ephesians that the believers would have.

Why is it so easy for us to listen to teachings about the cross and about "being broken"? Why is it easy to receive teachings on "learning lessons" and "being pressed"? It is because these things have existed in our concepts for a long time, and as a result, we do not need revelation regarding them. If you talk to monks and nuns about asceticism, they do not need any revelation and can understand immediately. If you speak to the Hindus about sufferings, they do not need revelation either. Without your repeated urging and charging, they have a clear understanding of self-mortification the moment you speak about it. When you speak to the followers of Confucius about seeking perfection in ethical pursuits or about character cultivation, you do not need to say too much to enable them to understand what you are saying because these things are already in them. When we speak concerning real spiritual things, however, we really need revelation. Without revelation it is difficult for us to understand them, and we immediately deviate from their original meaning.

If someone were to cover me with a big piece of cloth, and if I were to stand in front of you, you would see only a heap and would wonder what it was. You would likely be puzzled by this mystery. If the sheet were removed, you would still need light to see what was there. To remove the sheet is to unveil, to reveal; however, if there is no light and it is still dark, one still cannot see. Moreover, even if there is light, one who is blind still will not be able to see. Revelation plus light and sight enable a person to see a view. This is a vision.

The problem today is that within us we all have natural things, and these things are just like flypaper that one hangs to catch flies. When flies come, they stick to the flypaper immediately. The natural concepts within us are just like a sheet of flypaper. Anything that corresponds to them immediately gets stuck to them. Ephesians is full of revelations, such as the revelation concerning the unsearchable riches of Christ and the power of His resurrection, yet we do not care when we hear them. We do not pay much attention to revelation, because we are full of natural concepts within.

When a person is saved and comes into the church, immediately he has the thought that from that day onward he must behave properly. Then someone who has advanced a little may draw up some guidelines for him on how to be a proper Christian. The newly saved person will then try to be a Christian according to these guidelines. To do this requires neither teaching nor revelation. The thought that he must behave properly is already in him. This is often the case with those who listen to sermons. In fact, those who are preaching the sermons may not have any revelation either. They may preach from their natural concept, saying things such as: "Since we have been saved, we should glorify God in our daily walk." Actually there is no need to teach people such things, because this view has been in them since long before they were saved. Some preachers may go further to say, "We are too hard, so the Lord has to strike us and subdue us through the circumstances." When we hear this word, it sounds very logical, and it also corresponds with our concepts. In Christianity there are mostly natural teachings. There is almost no revelation.

The Bible is not without revelation, but when people read the Bible, they often touch only the surface, not the substance, the revelation. For example, Ephesians is altogether a book of revelation, but I can assure you that almost one hundred out of one hundred who read it do not see the revelations in it. What everyone sees is: Husbands, love your wives; wives, be subject to your husbands; children, honor your father and mother; and parents, do not provoke your children to anger. These items are just like flypaper. When you read them, you get stuck to them. Actually, people already teach these things even if they have not read about them. Yet regardless of how many times they read chapter one concerning the fullness of Christ, they cannot see it. This is like ink on marble—the marble simply cannot absorb the ink. It is also like writing on marble with a pen—no matter how hard we may try, we cannot write anything on it. We read about the fullness of Christ, yet this matter just slides away from us. We read about the creation of the one new man, yet it slides away. We read about the unsearchable riches of Christ and the great power within us, yet these matters also just slide away. However, when we come to 3:20a, which says, "To Him who is able to do superabundantly above all that we ask or think," immediately we are impressed. We might say, "Oh, I prayed to the Lord for a house with three bedrooms, and He has given me a house with five bedrooms. His grace is so great and is above all that I ask and think." This phrase *above all that we ask or think* will certainly be printed in us because we have asked and thought of many things. However, as to the latter half of this verse, which says, "According to the power which operates in us," after reading it a hundred times, we are still not impressed, because we do not have this thought in us. Similarly, concerning the phrase *to Him be the glory in the church* (v. 21a), we also may not see what this means after reading it a hundred times. When we come to chapter four, the easiest word to receive is, "He who steals should steal no more" (v. 28). We will surely be impressed by this. Actually, we do not even need to read the whole phrase. We get this thought just by reading half of the phrase. As a matter of fact, even without reading any of it, we already have this thought in us. However, we may read the verses containing the revelations in the book of Ephesians a hundred times and still not see anything. Therefore, many people can speak only about the matters in this book that are according to their natural concepts.

LETTING CHRIST, WHO IS ALREADY IN US, GROW AND SPREAD OUT OF US

Today in His recovery the Lord truly desires to bring His church into revelation. We all need to see a revelation. All man-made cultivation and improvement belong to Confucianism, Buddhism, gnosticism, and asceticism. They are not what God wants. Our eyes must be opened by God to see that Christ has come into us to be our all. Christ, who is our all, is already in us. If you see this revelation, you will realize that in a sense even eating the Lord is not necessary. In response to this statement, some may say, "Oh, this is a hard word; who can hear it? Are we supposed to eat the Lord or not?" It is true that for the body to grow, it is necessary to eat. There is no doubt about this. The Bible, however, also reveals that the Lord has sown Himself into us. In Matthew 13 the Lord spoke the parable of the sower. Strictly speaking, since the seed that was sown into the soil contains all the riches of life, eating is not necessary. What the seed needs is the opportunity to develop in the soil.

Every seed contains all the riches of its life, and every kind of life has three characteristics: its substance, its function, and its form. Suppose there is an apricot tree that is blossoming and bearing fruit. Do I have to worry that the apricots may grow and eventually take the shape of bananas? Do I need to ask an expert to make some apricot molds to cover the tiny apricots so that they will grow into beautiful apricots? No one would be so foolish as to do such a thing. I should simply go home and sleep. The apricot life contains the apricot shape. If I let the apricot life grow, eventually the apricot shape will come forth. Likewise, when a puppy is born, you do not need to make a mold in the shape of a dog and place it over the puppy so that it will grow and take the shape of a dog. You just need to let the puppy grow, and it will grow into its own shape.

Romans chapter eight speaks of being conformed to the image of the Son of God (v. 29). In the past when I gave messages along this line, I often told people that we need the circumstances to shape us. I likened this to the sisters placing dough into a mold after it has been kneaded when they are baking cakes or cookies. After the dough is beaten, kneaded, and pressed, a form emerges. Today, with regret I retract such a wrong teaching. The image of Christ does not come by outward molding but by the growth of His life within us. Christ's life has its substance and shape. Thus, if you let it grow in you, spontaneously the image of Christ will come forth. A peach tree will grow fruit bearing the shape of peaches, and an apricot tree will grow fruit bearing the shape of apricots.

A cat will grow into the shape of a cat, and a dog will grow into the shape of a dog. Since the life in you is the life of Christ, regardless of how you grow, you will never grow into the likeness of the devil. The life in you is the life of Christ. It is possible to prevent it from growing, but the more you allow it to grow, the more it will grow Christ. The substance, function, and shape are the riches that are contained in a seed. The seed contains all the riches of life. From this perspective, we can say that what is needed today is not for us to eat, but for us to allow the seed to develop.

We need to see the revelation that the seed has been sown in us. We also need to see that God does not want us to do anything or try to grow anything. God's intention is to sow Himself in His Son as a seed into us. He also wants the seed to grow out from us. This revelation is largely lacking in Christianity. Christianity as a whole has teachings concerning human conduct, asceticism, behavior improvement, and life in general, but it is short of revelation and does not see that these things are not what God wants. God's desire is to come into us in His Son, to be developed in us, and to be our all. We all need to see this revelation. Today I have a burden upon me to show the churches that God's chief desire is not that we would learn the lessons of the cross or receive the breaking of our flesh. His desire is not that we learn lessons and endure sufferings. Rather, His desire is to sow Christ into us that Christ may grow out from us.

THE NEED TO SEE REVELATION

What we have been touching in these messages is a matter of revelation. We have seen God's eternal plan, the all-inclusive Christ, the marvelous Spirit, and our spirit. In addition to these four visions, we also need to see clearly that God does not want anything from us. He does not want us to be broken, to improve our behavior, to learn lessons, to suffer, or to bear the cross. Rather, He wants Christ to be sown in us and to grow out of us. This is what He wants. We also need to see that the unsearchable riches, and the great power as well, are already in us. We need to see this.

Recently I fellowshipped with some brothers, saying, "To eat Christ we need to pray-read; to eat Christ we need to call on the Lord's name; to eat Christ we need to turn to our spirit; and to eat Christ we need to pray a great deal. However, suppose you did not have pray-reading, calling on the Lord's name, turning to the spirit, or praying. Then what would you do? In other words, suppose you were not allowed to pray-read, to call on the Lord's name, to turn to your spirit, or to pray, what would you do? Would you still eat Christ or not? Would you have a way to do this?" Here I appreciate the word *revelation*. If you do not have revelation, you would be finished in this situation. If you have the revelation—if you have seen clearly that Christ has been sown into you, that all the riches of Christ are in you, and that the great power is already in you—then the more you were prohibited from outward activities, the more you would appreciate this revelation. Do not misunderstand me. I am not saying that we should not pray, call on the Lord's name, pray-read, or turn to our spirit. I do not mean to say that we are now free and that we no longer need to do anything. We should not be this way. We all need revelation. If you have truly seen that Christ is in you, that the unsearchable riches of Christ are in you, and that the great power is in you, then the more you stop the outward activities, the better off you will be. Christ is a seed, and as such, He is living.

Farmers all know that when seed is sown into a field, the best thing to do is to ignore it. Suppose you loosen the soil today to take a look and to try to render a little help to the seed. The next day you do something else to try to help it somewhat, and then you try to pull on the sprout to help it grow. The result will be that the crop will be ruined. Similarly, the primary matter today is not pray-reading, eating and drinking, or turning to our spirit. Rather, it is giving Christ the opportunity to grow and spread in us. We do not need to receive anything anymore. All the riches are already in us. This is what Paul said: "For when I am weak, then I am powerful" (2 Cor. 12:10b). This was because when he was weak, he did not do anything; instead, he allowed the inner power to be expressed. This is revelation.

Do not misunderstand my words. It is correct that we need to pray-read, call on the Lord's name, turn to our spirit, and pray a great deal. All these things are right, and we really need them. Strictly speaking, however, the growth of Christ in us does not depend on these things directly; rather, it depends on the opportunity we provide for Him to expand in us. The problem is that, because we do not have a strong and clear revelation, although it seems that we understand, we really do not understand. If we are truly clear, we will need to pray-read more, but the nature of our pray-reading will no longer be the same. We will need to call on the Lord's name more, but the nature of our calling will be changed. We will need to turn to our spirit even more, but our turning now will be different from our turning before because we have seen the vision. Christ does not require us to do anything. He only wants us to give Him the greatest opportunity to spread in us.

In the previous message we used the gas station as an illustration of our relation to the Lord. However, this illustration is not so accurate. Since we have all the riches inside, what else do we need to be filled with? Once Christ comes into us, He is in us forever, and everything comes in with Him. It is not that today Christ comes into us with a little bit of Himself, then tomorrow He adds a little more, and the day after tomorrow He adds some more. Strictly speaking, it is not an adding but a spreading. Everything has already come into us. Now the question is, will we let Him spread? When we see a big peach tree with hundreds of peaches on it, do not forget that five years earlier the peach tree may have been only a seed. When that seed was sown into the soil five years earlier, fertilizer and water may have been added. However, in any case, the substance of life, the function of life, and the shape of life were all contained in that seed. After it has been sown into the soil, all that matters is whether it is given the opportunity to grow, and whether the riches inside are given the chance to develop fully. If you allow the seed to develop today, in five years you will have a tree full of peaches.

We all need to see a revelation. We need to pray, "O Lord, show me the revelations in Ephesians, and show me how Christ is the all-inclusive seed, how all His riches are in the seed, and how He has been sown in me." Within this seed there are the substance, the function (which is His great power), and the form (which is His image). Do we allow Him to expand in us, to develop all that He is, all that He has, and all that He can do? We definitely need to see the importance of this. When we minister to others, strictly speaking, it is not we who minister to them. We simply help them to see that Christ is already in them and that He needs the opportunity to spread out of them.

THE WASHING OF THE WATER IN THE WORD

Now let us consider a few verses from chapter five of Ephesians (vv. 25-27, 29). Ephesians is a book of revelations. In these few verses I will bring out only two points: one is the water in the word, and the other is nourishing and cherishing. These verses show us again that the church is the Body of Christ, and we all are members of the Body. Actually, our proper living is not a matter of learning lessons nor a matter of enduring sufferings and bearing the cross. Ephesians 5 reveals that we need the water in the word. There is water in God's word. The word here does not denote a lengthy discourse or the words printed in the Bible. The word here is the instant word, the present word, the word today. Two different Greek words are used in the New Testament for *word:* one denotes God's constant word and the other denotes God's instant word. The one used here in Ephesians 5 denotes God's instant word. The Bible is God's constant word. After we read it, however, it becomes the instant word to us. Many times the Lord also speaks an instant word directly within us. We may think that the Lord's words must be the words written in the Bible. Actually, it is not necessarily so, because the Lord who is in us is living, and He speaks to us. In principle, of course, the words which the Lord speaks to us within will never contradict His constant words in the Bible. However, in detail, numerous words that the Lord speaks to us throughout our whole life are not found in the Bible. For instance, when you are going to watch a movie the Lord may say within you, "Do not go to see that movie." No matter how hard you try, you will not be able to find this word—*Do not go to see that movie*—in the Bible. The Bible does not have this word, but actually in the Christian's experience of life, this kind of word may occur frequently. This is the instant word spoken of here in Ephesians 5.

The Lord's words contain the element of water, which simply speaking, is spirit and life. The Lord said, "The words which I have spoken to you are spirit and are life" (John 6:63b). In other words, the Lord's words have cleansing power. The water here is not for supplying but for cleansing, that is, for the cleansing and washing of the church. What is washed away is not defilements or sins, but spots and wrinkles. Wrinkles are related to oldness. You must let the water in the word, that is, the spirit and the life in the word, do a metabolic work in your organic being by adding new life elements into you to replace the old elements. This is a metabolic process and a discharging. We all know that metabolism takes place within us by which something new is supplied and added to us and something old is discharged and eliminated. This metabolism is the cleansing referred to in Ephesians 5.

Now you can see that no matter how much you tell people to learn the lessons of the cross, to be broken, and to endure sufferings, they can never experience metabolism by these things. This requires a revelation. When we help people, we should not try to teach them too much. If we do this, we will lead them into a maze. Instead, we should help them receive the Lord's instant word, the Lord's living word, every day. The spirit and the life contained in the Lord's living word will become the cleansing water that brings the life functions to their organic constitution.

Ephesians 5:26 says, "That He might sanctify her [the church], cleansing her...." According to the Greek grammatical construction of this verse, it is difficult to decide whether sanctifying or cleansing comes first. According to the grammar, these two things occur simultaneously. When the church is being sanctified, she is being cleansed, and when she is being cleansed, she is being sanctified. We know that to be sanctified is to have the element of the Holy Spirit added into us, and to be cleansed is to have the old elements discharged from us. Sanctification is an addition, whereas cleansing is a subtraction. What is added is Christ, and what is subtracted is our oldness.

The combination of these two—sanctifying plus cleansing, and cleansing plus sanctifying—is what is called transformation in the New Testament. As referred to in the New Testament, on the one hand, transformation is a sanctifying, and on the other hand, it is a cleansing. On the one hand, the element of Christ is added, and on the other hand, the element of Adam is eliminated. This is transformation. Wrinkles surely do not come from the element of Christ but from the old Adam. These things cannot be removed by the cross nor cleansed by the precious blood. We need Christ as the new element to be added into our organic constitution. When this happens, the elements of the old creation will be replaced.

FOR THE NOURISHING AND CHERISHING OF THE BODY

In addition to being cleansed, we also need to be nourished and cherished. Our body must receive nourishment. The ordinary way to nourish our body is for us to eat. To eat is to receive outward nourishment into our body so that it becomes our inner elements. The nourishing in Ephesians 5 is this kind of eating. Our body needs this kind of nourishing. It also needs to be cherished, to be kept warm. If you ask doctors, they will tell you that for most illnesses the body needs to be kept warm. If you are not kept warm, you become cold and stiff, and you may even die. The Greek word for *cherish* is difficult to translate. It means, on the one hand, to warm, and on the other hand, to soften. When we are cold, we become stiff and hard, and when a person dies, his body becomes stiff and cold. If any kind of hardness develops in any part of your body, that is bad because it might be a tumor. For the body to stay healthy, it must be nourished, and kept warm and soft. If we have a boil, that spot can become hard and cold. The lessons of the cross may cause people to become cold, and the breaking may cause them to become hardened. The more breakings they experience, the more they become hardened. Because you do not have any sores or boils on your body, your body is soft all over. Suppose, however, you are cut with a knife. After half an hour, both sides of the cut will become hardened. Being broken, receiving the cross, and enduring sufferings cannot keep us warm and soft. Today, what is really beneficial to our body is that which can warm and soften it. It is all right for our body to sweat, because we sweat when we are warm. However, do not expose yourself to coldness or you may catch a cold. In order to protect your body, it is better to keep it warm rather than to let it get cold.

Today we need to see these principles of life from the Lord's Word. When brothers or sisters live together, they should not make their homes seem like funeral homes. All the corpses in the funeral homes are stiff. When people visit a brothers' house, they should be able to sense the warmth there. They should be able to sense that everyone there is softened. If I come to visit your sisters' house, and when I step inside, the atmosphere is cold, everyone's face has an icy look, and nobody dares to say a word, then something is seriously wrong there. If I come to the brothers' or sisters' house, and the moment I enter, I can feel the warmth there, and if every one of you is soft when I speak with you, then I will know that the spiritual condition there is proper.

In Greek, the meaning of *nourishing* and *cherishing* implies feeding the body so that it is always kept warm and soft. Do not be like a corpse and become cold and rigid. Suppose a person who has been sick for a long time is about to die. When you touch his feet, you will feel that they are cold. After ten minutes the legs will be cold. After another ten minutes the coldness will reach his knees, and fifteen minutes later the coldness will reach his thighs. At that stage you know that he is about to die. As soon as a person dies, their whole body becomes cold. Some brothers and sisters have received the kind of "help" that makes them cold, then makes them hard, and finally causes them to became a stiff corpse. May the Lord have mercy on us and deliver us out of all these situations. The entire church life and all the church meetings should be in a nourishing and cherishing situation.

CHAPTER TEN

STANDING AND SLAYING

In this final message we want to look at the last chapter of Ephesians. Ephesians 6:10 says, "Finally, be empowered in the Lord and in the might of His strength." The Greek word for *empowered* has the same root as the word for *power* in chapters one and three. This power is a dynamo; it is an energizing power and an exploding power. Here the word is used in the verb form, which means "to be energized, to be made powerful." Hence, the proper rendering of this word is "be empowered."

Verse 11 says, "Put on the whole armor of God that you may be able to stand against the stratagems of the devil." Furthermore, verses 13 and 14a say, "Therefore take up the whole armor of God that you may be able to withstand in the evil day, and having done all, to stand. Stand therefore...." Verses 17 and 18 continue, "And receive the helmet of salvation and the sword of the Spirit, which Spirit is the word of God, by means of all prayer and petition, praying at every time in spirit and watching unto this in all perseverance and petition concerning all the saints."

Ephesians 3 tells us that the great power is already in us. Then, before the close of the book, chapter six tells us that we need to be empowered. Actually, we have already been empowered. We already have the power, but now we need to be strengthened by that power. Hence, chapter six is no doubt a continuation of chapter three. The power is not outside of us; it is in us. So now we need to be strengthened with this power.

STANDING IN THE VISIONS SEEN IN EPHESIANS

My burden in this message is to fellowship with you about

standing. If you have not seen the revelations in the first five chapters of Ephesians, I can assure you that you will not know where to stand. However, if you have seen what is in the first five chapters, from now on you need to stand. Where do you stand? Of course, you need to stand in the revelations seen in the first five chapters. Suppose after reading these messages, you begin to study other things. Once you do this, you may be pulled away by these things. Even without this, you may still fall away from the visions you have seen. Thus, you need to stand in the visions which you have seen.

You have seen the vision of God's eternal purpose, so you need to stand in God's eternal purpose. You have seen the vision of the all-inclusive Christ, so you need to stand in the all-inclusive Christ. You have seen the vision of the Spirit, so you need to stand in the Spirit. You have seen that the unsearchable riches of Christ and His great power are in you and that you do not need to use outward human effort to improve your behavior or to be broken. You have seen that what you need is to let Christ's riches and power be expressed through you. Since you have seen these things, you need to stand in them.

Keep in mind that in chapter one Paul did not speak about standing. If at the outset in chapter one, Paul had said, "You need to stand," then I would ask him, "Brother Paul, where do you want me to stand? Should I stand on the elementary lessons of character cultivation in Confucianism? Should I stand on the lessons of the cross?" The reason we do not have to ask him where we should stand is because he tells us clearly in the first five chapters. We need to stand in the fullness of Christ, which is the church. We need to stand in the new man, who is also the church. We need to stand in the visions we have seen.

Today many Christian preachers preach from Ephesians with a very natural view, saying, "Oh, brothers, make sure that you do not fall! As young people you are often tempted to go to the movies. Some may even try to persuade you to go to dancing parties. However, you need to stand! Stand by the might of the Lord's strength!" This is the kind of standing spoken of by Christians in general. It is a shame if we still speak of standing in this way. After all these messages, our eyes should be opened to see where we should stand. We should stand in our visions—in God's eternal purpose, in the all-inclusive Christ, in the unsearchable riches of Christ, and in the great power.

If others in the church still like to hear good sermons or messages, you need to stand and not be dragged down by them. Two days ago I heard someone share that the church is a restaurant. When I heard this, I said amen. Afterwards, however, I did not feel quite at ease inside. I would ask, "What do we eat in this restaurant?" If we eat a meal that is ordinary and plain, this is all right. However, if we eat sweet rice pudding every day, then soon we will be ready to be put in a coffin. When I went back to my room after hearing the sharing concerning the church being a restaurant, I could not sleep peacefully. Then last night someone said that since the church is a restaurant, it needs good cooks. I also felt uncomfortable when I heard this word. Finally, this morning when a sister was speaking lengthily on how we need good cooks, I was made clear by her speaking. I realized that all this speaking is trying to drag me back to religion. Eventually it will cause me to change in nature. I, however, have no intention to be a cook in a restaurant. Therefore, immediately I said to myself, "I must stand." We do not want restaurants! Down with restaurants! We do not want cooks! We do not want preachers! We do not want pastors preaching sermons! We do not want to eat at restaurants. We want to eat ordinary and plain meals at home. Who should cook? We all should cook for ourselves! Everyone has to do his own cooking. The church is not a restaurant. The church is a home. We eat ordinary and plain meals at home, and everyone cooks and eats for himself.

Our eyes must be opened. Do not let them become blurred. We must "be empowered in the Lord and in the might of His strength." We need to see through the stratagems of the enemy. In Matthew 16 Peter first told the Lord, "You are the Christ, the Son of the living God." This was revealed to him by the Father who is in the heavens (vv. 16-17). A short while later, however, he said, "God be merciful to You, Lord! This shall by no means happen to You!" (v. 22). This was Satan! A moment earlier Peter was in the heavens; a moment later he had become the devil. We must beware of the stratagems of the devil. I am not saying that what fallen Christianity preaches concerning standing is not the truth. I am saying that it is too low. Today we must see that Ephesians is not talking about filthy things such as dancing, playing cards, being seduced, and falling into temptations. What does Ephesians speak about? It speaks about the heavenly visions, such as the eternal purpose of God, the all-inclusive Christ, the unsearchable riches of Christ, the great power, and the abolishing of the ordinances through the cross. Ephesians does not speak only about the Lord's crucifixion for the redemption of our sins. It says that on the cross the Lord created the two—the Jews and the Gentiles—in Himself into one new man. The Jews and the Gentiles have all been crucified. We should stand in this! There are neither Greeks nor Jews, Chinese or Japanese in the church as the new man. In the church there is only the new man.

Let me test you again. From today onward, where will you stand? Suppose someone were to say to you, "We should stand on not losing our temper and on not playing mah-jongg." If they were to say this, you should reply, "Go away! This is a low preaching! Today I am standing in the visions in Ephesians. I do not need the low preaching." Suppose someone else were to say, "Our meetings have become lifeless, so we need to ask Brother So-and-so to come here." What would you say to this? You should not say "Go away!" to this. Instead, you should say, "I am standing!" Does saying this mean that you are proud? It does not. We must see something eternal, something exceedingly great—the mystery of God and the mystery of Christ. We must see that the all-inclusive Christ is in us, and every one of us must say, "O Lord, I will stand today!"

At this point I would like to ask you another question. Suppose that after you have declared that you will stand, the saints in the meetings gradually revert to sitting comfortably, then to sitting silently, and then eventually to sitting "deadly." If this happens, what will you do? At that time, the sisters should remind the brothers, saying, "Brothers, stand!" Someone else should rise and say, "Praise the Lord, I cannot sit any-more. I have a great power in me!"

I firmly believe that through these messages you have seen a vision and that something has entered into you. I abso-lutely believe that, even if you are willing to let yourself fall, and even if you were to jump into the lake of fire (needless to say this is impossible), you will bring with you what has been impressed into you, and no matter how much you try, you will not be able to get rid of it. Even if you regret what you have seen and want to get rid of it, it is too late. It is the Lord's mercy that He not only has shown us the heavenly visions but has also caused the visions to be branded into us so that, regardless of how hard we may try, we cannot wash them away. I absolutely believe that we will not be able to forget the visions that we have seen. Now we need to stand! We must stand in every local church!

SLAYING RELIGION WITH THE SWORD OF THE SPIRIT

Now let us go further to see a supplementary point, a point concerning spiritual warfare. In spiritual warfare we need to put on the whole armor of God, and the last two items in the armor of God are the helmet of salvation and the sword of the Spirit. Ephesians 6 says that we need to receive the helmet of salvation and the sword of the Spirit by means of all prayer and petition (vv. 17-18a). We must know that the helmet is for protection, and the sword is for slaying the enemy. These two items are very meaningful. On the one hand, we need protection, and on the other hand, we need to kill the enemy. In this message we will not say too much concerning the aspect of protection. When we are in our local-ities, we should say, "O Lord, put the helmet of salvation on us. Do not let Satan shoot the darts of natural concepts and of religious thoughts into our minds. O Lord, control our thoughts and our thinking. Preserve our minds." Our focus in this mes-sage is on the sword of the Spirit. The sword of the Spirit is for slaying. Several Bible translations indicate that the sword refers to the word of God. However, according to the Greek grammatical construction, the sword here is not the word of God but the Spirit. The Spirit is the sword, and the Spirit is also the word of God. In John 6 the Lord says, "The words which I have spoken to you are spirit and are life" (v. 63b). The word is the Spirit. Ephesians 6 reverses the order and says the Spirit is the word of God.

We must see that the word of God is the Spirit of God. You cannot separate the word of God from the Spirit of God. When I speak forth God's word, what goes out from me is the word, but it is the Spirit who enters into you. When the word is spoken again by you, it is the word, but when it enters into others, it is the Spirit again. The word is the Spirit, and the Spirit is the word. The two are one. What I speak here is the word, but what enters into you is the Spirit. The Spirit is the word, and the word is the Spirit. Thus, this word is not doctrine or knowledge. The Lord told us that His words are spirit. God's Spirit comes forth, and when we touch Him, He is the word. The Spirit is God's word.

In Ephesians 6 God's word is not for supplying but for killing, because it is the sword. What then does it kill? It kills anything that is contrary to God's vision. We are in a warfare. Anything that is contrary to the vision of God, the fullness of Christ, and the great power within us has to be slain. Do not tolerate it but slay it. You may have been trained and may have seen visions, but some of the other saints may still be in the old way. What shall you do? You need to kill. Do not kill the brothers and sisters, but kill the old way, kill the religious way, and kill the unwillingness to stand.

Perhaps two months after reading this, someone will come to you and speak some persuasive words, saying, "Look at your church here. There is neither speaking in tongues nor healing. What are you doing here?" Let me ask you, What shall you do? On the one hand, you need to stand, and on the other hand, you need to slay. Is this being too wild? It is not. Do you have to be polite to the enemy? We must stand and slay! As to ourselves, we need to stand, and as to the enemy, we need to slay.

YOUNG PEOPLE NEEDING TO BEAR
THE SPIRITUAL BURDEN OF THE CHURCH

Let us talk about our family affairs and consider our family.

Generally speaking, the churches everywhere, including the church in Taipei and the churches in Southeast Asia, are about the same—they all have some older ones and some younger ones. Most of the older ones are over sixty years of age. Those whom we refer to as younger ones are actually not that young. In our family tradition, everyone is considered a child until he is thirty-five years of age. If our family tradition had been changed ten or more years ago, today many of you would already be the core members of our family, because many of you are over twenty-three years old. According to the law of this country, twenty years old is considered the legal adult age. In the past our family tradition neglected this matter, so today many who are over twenty-two still behave like children who have no sense of responsibility toward their own family and who roam around freely outside.

Therefore, let us consider our family affairs. Is the church in your locality your home? Since we all would say that it is, since the fathers and mothers here are rather old now, and since the times have also changed, what shall we do? We need to reform. We should not revolt, but we should reform. How do we do this? The responsibility to do this is upon the young people. Every one of you should stand and slay. However, you must be careful. Do not kill your fathers and mothers or anyone else. Kill religion, and kill the old things. This killing is not fleshly but spiritual. In Ephesians 6 the sword used for killing the enemy is not the sword of the flesh but the sword of the Spirit. Your spirit must be strong, your spirit must be praying, and your spirit must execute the heavenly authority. Sometimes the older brothers and sisters, out of a good heart and intention, may propose to invite a preacher. By doing this, they unconsciously bring in religion. You do not need to oppose, but you need to stand in spirit. Do not slay the old ones who are the parents, and do not kill their proposals. Kill the enemy. In the meetings you need to pray in spirit and stand in spirit. You also need to rise up and share something one after another, sharing something that is fresh and full of supply. This will be like dropping a great number of bombs to completely demolish the old religion. This is the way to reform the church. None of the older ones in our home are our enemies. They all are our lovely parents. They love us, but it is not easy for them to get rid of their old concepts. Do not argue with them, because the more you argue, the more you will give room to the devil. Do not argue, and do not make a sound. Simply wait for the right time and then strike. If everyone stands up to release Christ and minister His riches, the older ones will say, "This meeting is really fresh! No wonder Brother Lee keeps declaring that this is really wonderful!" This will show that they have seen something. I believe that if you do this for half a year, your reformation will be a success.

Young brothers and sisters, the Lord's recovery is our big family, and you are its life pulse. These messages have a relaxed and easy manner, but I tell you, on my heart I bear a very heavy burden. All the churches, from Taipei to Indonesia in Southeast Asia, are too old. On the one hand, we thank the Lord that the churches are solidly for the Lord's recovery and for the Lord's unique ground. They are truly stable with regard to these matters. On the other hand, they are indeed too old. What then shall we do? I have considered this matter very much. If I go and speak these things again to the older brothers, they will nod their heads and receive my words. Their hearts may be more than willing to turn to a new situation, but their strength is lacking. Let me give you an illustration. I lack musical talent. Although I can select and call out hymns, when it comes to singing, I am like a person who can say but cannot do. When I was young, I was able to learn a little by humming the melody of a song a few times, but today not only can I not sing the new hymns, I cannot even manage to sing the old hymns. I am not the only one who is like this. All the older saints are about the same. If you do not believe me, let me ask four older brothers to sing for you. You will see that their singing is too poor. In this matter of singing, we who are older are hopeless. Even if you threaten to break us, crush us, and make hamburgers out of us, we still will not be able to sing well. However, if I were to ask four young people to sing for you, you would see how good their singing is. We who are older cannot sing. Regardless of how hard you press us, we cannot produce any oil. This is a clear illustration showing that the older ones should yield to the able ones, the young people. The older ones can stand behind them to supervise. They are our next generation, so we should turn our home over to them and let them take care of it. We should just stand on the side to watch. The young people have the vitality and are aggressive, yet they are not experienced. The older ones are more experienced, so they can watch on the side and render some help.

Therefore, from now on everyone must be clear that the housekeeping is the responsibility of the young people. Young people, you really need to go before the Lord and receive this burden from Him. I worship the Lord because your generation is made up of people who are in their twenties. Your generation is the cream of our family, and from now on you are the core of this big family. The future of this family completely hinges on you. Today in our home we still have the old fathers, old mothers, big brothers, and big sisters, so we do not need you to be responsible for many of the regular chores. What we expect of you is that on the spiritual side and in the meetings you would receive the baton. In the meetings you should not be proud, but you also do not need to be polite. You need to stand in spirit and bear the responsibility.

GIVING YOUR ALL TO AFFORD THE LORD A WAY

Does the Lord have a way to prepare His bride in today's Roman Catholic Church? The answer to this question is altogether a negative. It is impossible for Him to do this there. Can the Lord find a way to prepare His bride in today's Protestant churches? This is also impossible. Can the Lord find a way to prepare His bride in today's free groups? This is also impossible. Then where can the Lord go? By the Lord's mercy, it seems that He has a way in the Lord's recovery. If He still cannot find a way here, He will be forced to find another way. However, according to the situation today, and according to the prophecies, the time will not be delayed. Hence, I am convinced that today the Lord has a way in the church. He is preparing His bride here, and here He will usher in His coming again.

Therefore, young brothers and sisters, you must influence

all the churches on the whole island of Taiwan and all those in Southeast Asia as well. This is not a light matter. I hope that you will take this matter seriously to the Lord and receive the burden from His hand. I cannot give you the commission. I can only fellowship frankly with you according to the real situation and according to what I sense and know. I believe now you all are clear. May the Lord be gracious to you that every one of you will receive a sweet burden within. I would like to tell you that if I had one hundred lives, I feel it would be worthwhile to give them all for this way. I have been on this way for forty years, and I have never regretted it. Even up to this day I still feel glorious that I can be on this way. I repeat, if I had a hundred lives, I would lay every one of them on this way. May the Lord be merciful to us!

ABOUT THE AUTHOR

Witness Lee was born in 1905 in northern China and raised in a Christian family. At age 19 he was fully captured for Christ and immediately consecrated himself to preach the gospel for the rest of his life. Early in his service, he met Watchman Nee, a renowned preacher, teacher, and writer. Witness Lee labored together with Watchman Nee under his direction. In 1934 Watchman Nee entrusted Witness Lee with the responsibility for his publication operation, called the Shanghai Gospel Bookroom.

Prior to the Communist takeover in 1949, Witness Lee was sent by Watchman Nee and his other co-workers to Taiwan to insure that the things delivered to them by the Lord would not be lost. Watchman Nee instructed Witness Lee to continue the former's publishing operation abroad as the Taiwan Gospel Bookroom, which has been publicly recognized as the publisher of Watchman Nee's works outside China. Witness Lee's work in Taiwan manifested the Lord's abundant blessing. From a mere 350 believers, newly fled from the mainland, the churches in Taiwan grew to 20,000 in five years.

In 1962 Witness Lee felt led of the Lord to come to the United States, settling in California. During his 35 years of service in the U.S., he ministered in weekly meetings and weekend conferences, delivering several thousand spoken messages. Much of his speaking has since been published as over 400 titles. Many of these have been translated into over fourteen languages. He gave his last public conference in February 1997 at the age of 91.

He leaves behind a prolific presentation of the truth in the Bible. His major work, *Life-study of the Bible*, comprises over 25,000 pages of commentary on every book of the Bible from the perspective of the believers' enjoyment and experience of God's divine life in Christ through the Holy Spirit. Witness Lee was the chief editor of a new translation of the New Testament into Chinese called the Recovery Version and directed the translation of the same into English. The Recovery Version also appears in a number of other languages. He provided an extensive body of footnotes, outlines, and spiritual cross references. A radio broadcast of his messages can be heard on Christian radio stations in the United States. In 1965 Witness Lee founded Living Stream Ministry, a non-profit corporation, located in Anaheim, California, which officially presents his and Watchman Nee's ministry.

Witness Lee's ministry emphasizes the experience of Christ as life and the practical oneness of the believers as the Body of Christ. Stressing the importance of attending to both these matters, he led the churches under his care to grow in Christian life and function. He was unbending in his conviction that God's goal is not narrow sectarianism but the Body of Christ. In time, believers began to meet simply as the church in their localities in response to this conviction. In recent years a number of new churches have been raised up in Russia and in many eastern European countries.

OTHER BOOKS PUBLISHED BY
Living Stream Ministry